BATTLING THE BLUES

BATTLING THE BLUES
DARIUS BOYD

with **MICHAEL CRUTCHER**

FOREWORD BY WAYNE BENNETT

hachette
AUSTRALIA

Note from Darius: The semi colon on the spine of this book is a reminder that a mental health illness may pause your life, but it does not have to be a full stop. It is not the end. The semi colon is a symbol that reminds me there is always hope and help available if I am struggling. There are contact details at the back of the book that could assist you or someone you love.

Published in Australia and New Zealand in 2020
by Hachette Australia
(an imprint of Hachette Australia Pty Limited)
Level 17, 207 Kent Street, Sydney NSW 2000
www.hachette.com.au

10 9 8 7 6 5 4 3 2 1

 A catalogue record for this book is available from the National Library of Australia

ISBN: 978 0 7336 4572 3 (paperback)

Cover design by Christabella Designs
Front cover image courtesy AAP Image/Dan Peled
Back cover image courtesy Libby Willis
Images in picture section from Darius Boyd's collection unless otherwise credited
Typeset in Adobe Garamond Pro by Kirby Jones
Printed and bound in Australia by McPherson's Printing Group

 The paper this book is printed on is certified against the Forest Stewardship Council® Standards. McPherson's Printing Group holds FSC® chain of custody certification SA-COC-005379. FSC® promotes environmentally responsible, socially beneficial and economically viable management of the world's forests.

For Kayla, Willow and Romi.
You are what life is all about.

CONTENTS

GRATITUDE 2015–

Foreword

COMMITMENT IS A COMMON ATTRIBUTE AMONG MANY OF the great players I've coached. Commitment means struggle, sacrifice, effort, discipline and, at times, disappointment. It means no excuses. But not every athlete is committed. Some are just involved. They play extremely well, they can be game-winners, but that doesn't mean they are truly committed.

Great teams need committed men and Darius Boyd is one of the most committed men I've known.

I first met Darius a few months after his eighteenth birthday. He was introduced to me by the great talent scout Cyril Connell. He was one of the last players Cyril scouted for the Brisbane Broncos. He told me to be patient with Darius. He had a good build but he was a bit thin. He was a bit shy. And he didn't say much.

When I saw Darius on the training paddock, the first thing I noticed was his athleticism. He was a wonderful athlete. He had a great running style, he could move and step and he had tremendous speed. But I had seen a few of those players over the years and that didn't mean they were committed.

I had my first glimpse of Darius's commitment when we headed off for our pre-season camp before Christmas 2005. We had a new performance director who was about to make his mark on the team. The camp was followed by weeks of exhausting training sessions in the Brisbane summer. Darius stood up to it all. Bodies of young men aren't used to that level of work. Darius hung in with it the whole way and never complained once.

That made me think we had found a talented kid. He played in our pre-season games, although he was a bit tentative and he dropped a few balls. But he showed enough that we wanted to stick with him. You only had to tell Darius something once and he would get it. He stopped making errors and he became less tentative as he gained confidence. He watched the older players very closely and he took everything in, especially from Darren Lockyer. He bolted on to Locky early and learnt as much as he could from him.

But there was a lot more to Darius than his performances on the football field. I learnt a lot about him in our thirteen seasons together in the NRL. He's always been honest. I've asked him some hard questions and he's never told a lie. He's introverted and he's shy but he's never been that way around me. He built strong friendships in his teams which was always a good sign. If they don't have mates in the team then you do worry about them.

He didn't have a dad and no one can replace a dad. I never saw our relationship in that way but, if anything, I helped him in the same way that men helped me. I didn't have a father for most of my life but other men kept an eye out for me. I always tried to repay that to others.

I noticed early that Darius was putting on a brave front all the time. Given his upbringing, he was very good at masking his emotions. The smart ones are good at doing that because they don't want to risk all the progress they have made. They want to survive so they do what they need to do.

Rugby league helped Darius to survive but it also started to bring about his personal wars. He was always trying to be a perfectionist but being perfect was of course never attainable. After he had won the Clive Churchill Medal for St George Illawarra in the 2010 NRL grand final, he apologised to me. 'Sorry, Coach,' Darius told me in the change rooms. 'I made too many errors out there tonight.' The Dragons supporters, cherishing their first premiership in three decades, would have disagreed.

That pursuit of perfection was one of the signs of trouble. Darius found it hard to be pleased. He would play a great game and still be down. We went from the Dragons to Newcastle together and the walls closed tighter on him. That's where I first started to see the extent of his struggles. He was very angry with how he was playing and I could see the deterioration. We were in the gym one day and he was in a really bad way. He was even angry with me. He had never been like that with me. He was fighting a lot of demons.

The nineteenth-century author Robert Louis Stevenson once wrote: 'Sooner or later, everyone sits down to a banquet of consequences.' Darius had been masking his troubles for some time and his banquet had arrived. The bottom line was that he needed some help. And he was strong enough to ask for the help and to admit that he had some problems.

He left rugby league for a mental health clinic that did a wonderful job of listening to his story and helping him. They taught him that perfection wasn't attainable. But excellence was possible. I went to the clinic and noticed the change in him straight away. In his room, he said more to me that day than he had ever said to me at any other time. I can remember the scene. Darius was sitting on his bed, looking comfortable and relaxed. He said: 'Coach, I thought I had really serious mental issues but I've seen people who are really doing it a lot tougher than me. I have problems and I need to deal with them but I now know some people are doing it really tough.'

Darius became much calmer and more at ease with himself as a bloke. He didn't hide behind doors. He brought it out into the open. He came straight out with it. That's when he began to stop some of the wars going on inside him. And he began to talk about mental health widely in speaking engagements with people he'd never met before. He would relive it and he would relive it for the benefit of others.

He returned to football nine months later at the Broncos, where we had both moved after the 2014 season. He would soon become captain of the club that he always loved. The shy, introverted kid became a very good captain. He wasn't a natural leader but he learnt from the likes of Locky to make himself one. He became much more talkative and he gave good advice. He knew about human emotions because he'd been through so many of them leading the life that most of us don't want to live. He was only going to get better as a captain when the job was taken from him.

His behaviour has always been very good. He has always played the game in the right spirit. He's never made a cheap shot. He's never been to the judiciary. He's never upset anyone.

Darius's career has been remarkable: two premierships; a Clive Churchill Medal; a World Club Challenge win; ten State of Origin series and he won nine of those; twenty-three Tests and he won all of those including a World Cup final; and then you throw in his club career with fifteen seasons and more than three hundred games.

With a career like that, he should be a household name. He's done it all. But he's not a household name and that's because he always undersold himself. But that doesn't worry him.

He's different from any other footballer I've coached. He wasn't the rough, tough guy who would go out and want to tear the football field up and settle scores with blokes. That wasn't him. He wanted to be a footballer and he did it in a different way from most.

I don't know what Darius would have become if he wasn't a rugby league player. That's what I love about our game. He had a great teacher at his school in Rod Patison who helped him immensely. Darius came to the Broncos and he had players like Shane Webcke, Brad Thorn, Petero Civoniceva and Locky who were all very good men. He had some bad luck in his young days but he also had some good luck too getting around blokes like them. The right people helped him enormously and he's such a good observer that he took it all in.

Darius is still learning now. He's still growing as a person. He has got the most out of his playing career but there is a lot more to life after that. And that's what matters the most. Football is good but I want my players to have good lives.

Parenting has been a big game-changer for him and he's handled it beautifully. He was happy and proud to be a dad and to be a husband to Kayla. To see him with his daughters now is a wonderful thing. The love and affection he has for those girls is a special thing.

After football, Darius will do anything that he wants to do. He's a pretty special guy in that way. He'll make it work in ways that others can't.

When I left the Broncos at the end of 2018, I left Darius in the NRL for the first time. I felt good about that because I knew he didn't need me anymore. He had grown up.

The American football coach Vince Lombardi said many great things, including this: 'If you will not settle for anything less than your best, you will be amazed at what you can achieve in your life.'

Darius Boyd has never settled for anything less than his best. He's authentic. He's committed. That's what makes him.

He's definitely one of a kind.

Wayne Bennett, July 2020

Introduction

Wednesday, 23 December 2015

Been really struggling the last few days. I don't want to be angry and unhappy around Xmas time. It's just been really hard to snap out of it. I have been thinking really bad thoughts lately. Just been feeling really worthless. I don't think I would ever try to take my life. But when you feel so low sometimes it actually sounds like a good idea. Sometimes I feel like I'm fine and nothing is wrong. But then when I get like this, I realise I'm lying to myself. I just can't handle any little negative things. I let things get to me too easily. I need to remember what is important. And it's not little things or things that go wrong.

I have so much to be grateful for!!
BREATHE/SMILE
XMAS!!

That's from my journal. I kept it for eighteen months, writing my thoughts as I struggled through the darkest times of my life. Inside that small book with the brown cover were pages of raw emotion. I wrote about my faltering marriage, my relationship with my estranged mother, the deteriorating health of my beloved grandmother and the arrival of my first child. Most of all, I wrote about my feelings as I tried to improve my mental health after years of ignoring the pain in my life.

That journal contained very little mention of my football career. Rugby league had become a contributing factor to my depression. Until then, rugby league was my safe haven, where I would go to pretend that everything was well in my life. When my wife, Kayla, rang me in early July 2014 to tell me that she was leaving me, I was in a State of Origin training camp with the Queensland Maroons.

'Okay,' I told Kayla. 'If that's what you think is best.'

It was the cold response of someone out of touch with reality. A few nights later, I ran on to Suncorp Stadium in front of 52 000 roaring fans and scored a try in a Queensland victory over New South Wales. How can life be bad when you have so many people cheering you on? I lived my life within the boundaries of a football field rather than the real world. I returned home after that State of Origin match to an empty house. Years of ignoring my mental health were catching up with me. I played two more games of rugby league and checked into a clinic to begin plotting a way out of the darkness.

For a few days, it was the most popular story in Australian sport – Darius Boyd had walked away from football because of mental health problems. The media asked how many other players were carrying the same burden but refusing to face up to it? Did athletes need sympathy or did they need to toughen up? Was it really possible to feel sorry for someone earning plenty of money when so many people were struggling in their lives?

In the clinic, I was given a series of tips to help me in my recovery. One of the first things I did was to start a journal that would become a record of my feelings and my progress. I would be able to read back through the journal to remember how far I had come since admitting that I needed help. I wrote the goals for my recovery inside the front cover:

Be happier – SMILE

Enjoy life

Do charity work

Put family first

Be more social

Try new things

Talk about things more

Help out with anything

The journey would take a while and it wouldn't be without tough times. The next twelve months threw up some moments of real joy: Kayla generously gave me another chance; our treasured daughter Willow was born; I reconnected with my mother after not speaking with her for more than eight years; I returned to play with my beloved Brisbane Broncos; Queensland won a State of Origin series; and I was part of a Broncos team that played in one of the most nail-biting grand finals in the National Rugby League's modern history, although we lost in extra time. But the bumps in the road kept coming and, on 23 December 2015, I wrote the most despairing entry in my journal.

I never wrote again in that journal. I should have written in it plenty of times to keep track of my progress but life with a young family became busy. Despite that, I continued to focus on gratitude. I made an effort to get more involved in the community. I tried doing new things, like talking to people I didn't know well, although that didn't come easily. I even began public-speaking lessons. I reminded myself to smile more often. Importantly, I tried not to let little things worry me, including criticism from people I didn't know.

This is my extended journal, looking back at the long path from depression to gratitude, and all that happened in between. Knowing there would always be challenges in life, I scribbled down in one section of that journal a piece of advice for when times were tough:

I need to look at the bigger picture. My goals, my beliefs, my standards. I know I can be so, so happy and that's the person I want to be. EVERYTHING HAPPENS FOR A REASON. I CAN AND WILL BENEFIT FROM THIS!

ANXIETY
1987–2005

CHAPTER 1

The Boyds

MY FIRST MEMORIES ARE GRAINY. A CHOCOLATE CAKE IN A rectangle shape decorated with chocolate frogs and Smarties. It was my fourth birthday and my family were helping me to celebrate. There is a photo of that day that I treasured for many years. My mum, Rochelle Boyd, was smiling. My grandmother Delphine and my grandfather Herbie were beaming in their party hats. I had the biggest smile for Dallyn in this photo. Dallyn was my uncle but he was also a father figure to me, a fun-loving guy who was always playing jokes. As a young bloke, I would often be at my grandparents' house on the Gold Coast waiting for Dallyn to arrive for a visit from Brisbane. Delphine, who I called Nana, would tell me when Dallyn was about to arrive and I would go to the window and wait excitedly, only to watch him drive straight past the house.

'Oh no, he's forgotten where we live again,' Nana would tell me.

I would bolt downstairs, waving my arms to attract Dallyn's attention before guiding him into the driveway like a desperate air-traffic controller on the tarmac, making sure he found the house. Dallyn would jump out of the car with a huge smile and rub his hands through my hair as I asked him incredulously how he could continue to forget the house in which he and my mum had grown up.

Mum. Nana. Pa. Uncle Dallyn. They were my family as I grew up on the Gold Coast, a happy kid with great memories of my early years. I had no dad and no siblings but that wasn't a problem for me. I lived with my mum but I loved my grandparents' house at Worongary on the edge of the hinterland. They had a two-storey house on acreage that was every young boy's dream. There was a creek at the back almost always filled with water and surrounded by plenty of stones to throw until my arms got tired. There were fruit trees with juicy pears that could be picked and eaten. There was a ride-on mower, which Pa took me for hundreds of joyrides on. And out the front was a cul-de-sac that was perfect for riding my bike for hours on end. The neighbours had a son the same age as me who joined me on plenty of adventures.

Nana had a sewing room at the back of the house. She was a dressmaker and was brilliant with her sewing machine. She would make me clothes that I thought were better than anything we could buy at the shops. She would take one of my plain T-shirts and transform it with a Teenage Mutant Ninja Turtles patch that I would then proudly wear to preschool. She was a simple woman with a taste for classical music.

Nana was also a terrific reader of bedtime stories, and I can still remember some of the books she would read to me as I tried my hardest to stay awake until the last page. Most of all, Nana was a caring grandmother who made me feel safe and loved, and kept me full of food.

A lot of that food was prepared by Pa Herbie, who performed very well in the kitchen at a time when you were lucky to find men who knew how to boil an egg. Nana and Pa had a servery in their kitchen, where I would stand and bang my hand on the counter while awaiting another treat thanks to Pa's excellent cooking skills. Pa was constantly cracking jokes and was always up for a game of cards or Monopoly. I won my fair share of card games but I'm pretty sure Pa let me win. I still love playing cards. These were happy times in my life and I treasure the memories.

But I was about to get my first realisation that life wasn't all one long journey of fun. I knew from a young age that my uncle Dallyn wasn't always well. He had first been diagnosed with a brain tumour when he was eight years old and he continued to fight recurring tumours throughout his life. They didn't stop him from living his life, moving to Brisbane and working at a large car dealership. He lived on Brisbane's southside so he could easily travel to the Gold Coast to spend time with us. It's funny what you remember when you look back on your early years. I recall that I loved Promite and hated Vegemite – you can really only like one of them – while Dallyn, like most Australians, loved his Vegemite. One day we were preparing to visit Dallyn in hospital, so Nana told me to make some sandwiches for my uncle. She thought it would be fun to play a trick on him so we put Promite on them and told Dallyn that it was his favourite, Vegemite. I remember the scene he put on as he bit into the sandwich only to find that it was Promite: his face contorted, he pretended to choke and he eventually spat out the sandwich. I thought it was hilarious. I remember that visit vividly because it would be among the last times I would see Dallyn. He was dying from his brain tumours, and he knew it. Yet whenever I turned up to see him in hospital, even in his final days, he found the energy and selflessness to make me laugh. His was a generosity that I will never forget.

I was devastated when Dallyn died. He was only thirty-six. I was eight. I had lost the closest thing I had to a father and the uncle who had meant so much to me in my early years. I remember sobbing after hearing the news. I can still recall the pain of that loss. I had never encountered death before, let alone of someone who meant so much to me. As a kid, you tend to think of yourself first. It was only years later, when I had my own children, that I would think back on that time and imagine the pain Nana, Pa and my mum must have felt at Dallyn's death.

The loss of Dallyn took a toll on Pa. He had been suffering from emphysema for many years due to the smoking that had been a part of life for his generation. Pa had been a police officer throughout his working life, mostly based on the Gold Coast. He and Delphine had been together from an early age. Nana's father was also a police officer, so she had some idea of what to expect when she married Pa. They were a close couple who celebrated the arrival of Dallyn at a relatively late age – Nana was thirty when Dallyn was born. They were unable to have a second child so, six years after Dallyn was born, Nana and Pa adopted my mum, Rochelle.

I can't imagine how tough it was for them to learn that Dallyn had a brain tumour at such a young age. But the Boyds always seemed to put their heads down and charge on without much fuss.

Mum was happy for me to find my own interests in life, like footy and athletics. She was a good mum when I was young, doing well to raise me while juggling jobs, including nursing, cleaning and a stint as the 'lollipop lady' helping kids across the pedestrian crossing at my school. She played social tennis once a week and had a small but tight-knit group of friends. Mum was relatively quiet, although she knew how to raise her voice if I was stepping out of line. To a young bloke, my mum seemed as normal as any mum. She worked hard to make sure I had things that my mates had. I received good presents for birthdays and Christmas, I had a PlayStation console, I had money to go to representative rugby league carnivals which were not cheap. They were material things, but as a young bloke I had no doubt that Mum loved me and did the best she could.

When I was a little kid I don't think I ever asked Mum who my father was. I'd never had a father so I didn't know any different. Mum was seriously involved with one guy, which prompted us to move to the Beaudesert region, about one hour's drive west of the Gold Coast, for about a year when I was six. Mum became engaged and even changed our surnames before the marriage. I'm not sure why she did that but I have proof of it – a junior trophy belonging to Darius Trevathan. That was my name for the year that I lived in Beaudesert. Life takes you on all sorts of journeys – it was lucky for me that we moved to Beaudesert because it was Mum's fiancé who introduced me to footy as a young kid. I'm thankful that he took an interest in me and encouraged me to play footy. Who knows if I would have played otherwise? I started in rugby union, wearing the blue, black and white of the Beaudesert Warriors for one season. I loved it from the first time I played. I remember enjoying rugby union because I was quick, but there was no tackling – you had to tag someone on the shorts with two hands to stop them. I just wanted to tackle. One of my mates at school told me that rugby league allowed its young players to tackle. That sounded superb to me. I wanted to have a crack at it and that's what sparked my move into the great game.

It was unfortunate that Mum's engagement broke down and she never married. I was in Year 2 and we headed back to the Gold Coast to resume our life not far from my grandparents' house. Dallyn's death had been devastating for them. Pa's health continued to deteriorate due to the emphysema, forcing him to rely on an oxygen bottle and make frequent visits to hospital.

After coming out of hospital one Friday afternoon, Pa visited Mum and me in the house where we were living. He was towing his oxygen bottle, but was heading home, rather than back to hospital, which I thought was a good sign. Like Dallyn, Pa wanted me to be happy, and I remember vividly that Friday afternoon though it was years ago and I was only eleven. It would be the last time I would see Pa. When Mum picked me up from school the next Monday afternoon, she told me that Pa had died in his sleep the previous night. It was a crushing blow to a young bloke without a father. First Dallyn had died and, three years later, Pa was taken away.

I don't remember being angry at the time. I remember the tears and the acute pain of losing Dallyn and Pa. It hurt a lot. But I don't remember anger. In years to come, I would look back on this time differently. I don't remember how Mum and Nana coped with it – I'm sure that they were devastated, but they were being brave for me. Those deaths would start a chain of events that would have a lasting impact on my life.

The first change was immediate – I began to narrow my thinking to focus solely on the things I really enjoyed: rugby league, athletics and my PlayStation console. They became my priorities because they gave me joy. Everything else would be blocked out or tossed aside. Call it a fool's paradise, because that's what it was, but it was my survival method and it had short-term benefits. It enabled me to stay afloat mentally and it helped me to develop skills in the activities I enjoyed. I had no idea of the long-term ramifications; they would be severe. With my shutters up, I also began to have problems with trust. This would become a long-term issue for me.

My grandmother moved out of the family home and into a townhouse. I dearly missed those times playing in the creek or picking fruit from the trees or riding my bike up and down the cul-de-sac. Christmases came and went and the photos we took show a stark difference from the ones taken of our celebrations in the past. Pa and Dallyn were gone and the photos of our family at Christmas seemed to follow a trend – the huge smiles I had in my younger days were replaced by looks of indifference. The photos charted my changing mood as I reached my teenage years. I know adolescence is a tough time for any kid, so maybe I shouldn't read too much into it, but I recognise now that I was starting to miss my grandfather and uncle – and a father figure in general – in ways that I didn't understand at that age.

It was about that time that I started to ask Mum what she knew about my father. This would prove to be the one question about my life that couldn't be answered. The reality was that Mum didn't know the identity of my father. She was twenty-two years old when I was born and she wasn't in a relationship. As my footy career developed, journalists would write about the fact that I didn't know who my father was. At the time, it seemed a bigger deal for the newspapers than it was for me. But the coverage led some people to contact me, or the clubs I played for, speculating on my father's identity. Someone emailed the Broncos early in my career to say that they were on a cruise ship with my mum in the year before my birth and that they knew my father was Polynesian. When I look in the mirror, I don't see any Polynesian features looking back at me. I didn't give that one too much thought. There was another person who got in touch via a friend's social media account to say that he was my father and to ask them to pass on that information. He even attached pictures of himself claiming that the similarities were obvious. He didn't look anything like me but I underwent a blood test just to be sure that he wasn't my father. And then there were three sisters who approached me through my then coach Wayne Bennett. They told me about how their dad knew my mum back before I was born and that they were sure they were my half-sisters. The story didn't sound crazy and they were so adamant that I agreed to undergo another blood test to see if they were right. The test came back negative.

My dad is out there somewhere. It would be nice to know his identity. What was he like? Where was he from? Was he tall and athletic? My mum is close to 1.8 metres tall and was a good tennis player so maybe my height and coordination came from her. Who knows? Were my mental health struggles passed on through my father or were they similar to the struggles that affected my mum? Maybe my dad liked playing footy, too. I do know that not knowing my father hasn't torn me up as much as some people believe. Yes, it would be great to meet him for so many reasons. But there's nothing I can do about that and I've resigned myself to it. I am at peace with that.

Around the time I began asking about my father, I became aware that my mother had been adopted by Nana and Pa. I wasn't old enough to understand the impact of not knowing my father or two of my grandparents. Mum tracked down her birth mother when I was about to become a teenager. She learnt that she had been born to a teenage mother, whom she eventually traced to a Queensland town. Mum found she had brothers and sisters whom my biological maternal grandmother had raised herself. I didn't know the identity of Mum's father. I was pleased for Mum that she had met the woman who gave birth to her. I can't imagine that it was easy to give up a baby, despite being so young at the time. My biological maternal grandmother and some uncles and aunties made some efforts to get involved in my life but I wasn't ready for that. My family had been Mum, Nana, Pa and Dallyn. I didn't have the capacity at that age to bring more people into my family, even if they were related. I was growing closer to Nana as I got older and was really treasuring my time with her. Nana struggled a bit as Mum began to spend more time with her natural mother. It wasn't an easy period for any of us. But there were harder days ahead.

CHAPTER 2

Studying for sport

MY GRANDMOTHER DELPHINE HAD A STORY SHE TOLD ME many times. When I was eight years old, Nana asked me what I wanted to do when I was older. 'I'm going to be a rugby league player,' I answered. That didn't fill Nana with confidence. As a woman born in the early days of the Great Depression, Nana wasn't thrilled when her only grandson told her his future lay in a career that was barely full time for most players. Nana would have preferred to hear me talk about a profession, a trade or something else that would sustain me for the many decades of work that lay ahead. But she would never discourage me – that was one of the reasons that she was so important to my life.

When I told Nana that I wanted to play rugby league, it wasn't because I didn't like school. I really enjoyed it. School was made for children who thrived on routine, structure and benchmarks – it was all about improving yourself and you received marks from exams to indicate how you were going. That was a great combination for me. I enjoyed learning and relished the challenge of improving and keeping my grades at a good level. But aside from rugby league, the only other career I considered was being a chef. I have always loved cooking – I got that from my grandfather – and I even took a cooking subject at school that I really enjoyed. For a while I thought about becoming a chef when I reached age fifteen and hadn't yet cracked a place on a junior Queensland representative rugby league team. Footy wasn't looking like a great career option despite my passion for the game.

I tried other sports over the years but without great success. I signed up for karate because I loved watching movies featuring Jean-Claude Van Damme and his helicopter kicks and splits; however, I went to my first karate lesson and copped a flogging. I never went back. I wasn't very good at cricket so that wasn't going to happen for me. I messed around with tennis and I loved running, so I began little athletics one summer, which I really enjoyed. I was a good sprinter until I worked out that the kids I could keep up with in the summer would put lengths on me during the winter while they kept training and I kicked a footy. I shifted to field events like discus and javelin and qualified for the national schools titles, but Mum couldn't afford to send me away to compete.

No sport ever came close to rugby league for me. I couldn't wait for the next footy season to come around. When Mum and I returned to the Gold Coast after our time in Beaudesert, I prepared to play league. My local club at Nerang didn't have a spot for me in their Under 8 team, so I went to the Parkwood Sharks who kitted me up and had me ready to go for the first game. While playing for Parkwood, I met a player called Steve Michaels. We would become great friends and play together for the Broncos in my first season in NRL. By the time I started playing rugby league, I was taking a real interest in the Brisbane Broncos. I would watch every game I possibly could on television and sometimes Mum would take me on the train to watch the Broncos play. That was a huge treat, walking in with thousands of Broncos fans to watch my team play. Wendell Sailor was my favourite player ahead of Darren Lockyer, who made his debut for the Broncos the year that I turned eight. How could I not be a Broncos fan in that era? They won premierships when I was aged five, six, ten, eleven and thirteen. Every kid loves a winner and I loved the Broncos.

I continued playing for Parkwood until I reached the Under 12s and the Sharks no longer had enough players to form a team, so I switched to the Mudgeeraba Redbacks for three seasons. Again, the Redbacks didn't have enough players to form a team when I reached the Under 15s so it was off to the Burleigh Bears, where I would take my first steps to senior football in a few years time.

During this time, Mum and I continued to move around. When I was young, Mum and I had flatted with one of her friends for a few months. Mum would find a way to keep us together in our own house as she worked her collection of jobs. When I was thirteen, Mum worked a job every Sunday night, which meant that she wouldn't get home until about

8 p.m. That was way too late for a hungry thirteen-year-old boy to wait for dinner, so Mum would let me cook up some sausages for myself while I watched television. She would bring me home dessert, which I always appreciated.

It was around this time that Mum's behaviour changed. She became quite emotionless and seemed distant towards me. I remember feeling like I was talking to someone I didn't know. I had no idea what was happening to Mum but, looking back on it now, I see that she was suffering from depression. Mum's mental health slowly deteriorated over two years. She began claiming she was in acute pain and needed to go to hospital immediately. I remember an ambulance coming to our house at about 2 a.m. after Mum had called in an emergency. I clearly remember the ambulance officers telling Mum that they couldn't find anything wrong with her but that they would take her to hospital if that's what she wanted. One night, I put my foot down and told Mum she wasn't going to hospital. She had already been to hospital three times and, once I heard the ambulance officer say that he thought she was fine, I didn't want us to go a fourth time. I was emotional, struggling to deal with the situation as a fifteen-year-old without much of an idea of how the world worked. I felt I was losing another family member because Mum wasn't the same Mum I remembered so fondly.

A few weeks later, I was at a friend's place for a sleepover. Mum checked herself into a mental health facility the same night. I had no idea that she had planned to leave home. What followed was a tumultuous time. I couldn't stay at home on my own and Nana wasn't in a position to look after me. She was unable to drive at night, which made it tough for her to take me to footy training a few nights a week. As a result, my one-night sleepover at my mate's place became a six-month stay when Mum decided to stay in the facility at Robina. I had two beloved dogs at that time: MacGyver, an eight-year-old cattle dog–staffy cross, and Tigger, her six-year-old son. As I had no siblings, those dogs were really important to my early life. Mum feared she couldn't look after them when she checked into the facility, so she had them put down. That was a devastating blow for me. Those dogs had followed me everywhere and I had had great fun playing with them as pups and as they became older.

Those six months sparked a lot of anger in me and created a deep resentment towards Mum. I couldn't understand what was happening in her life. She came out of the mental health facility after six months and we moved back in together, our relationship forever changed. But Mum didn't last long at home before she returned to the facility. I went back to my mate's house for another few months with his family very generously helping me out again. After that, I moved in with Nana for my last year of school. I visited Mum a few times in the mental health facility and it was an uncomfortable experience. Looking back on it, Mum showed courage to check herself into the facility. She didn't have the support of a partner and Nana was still grieving the deaths of her husband and son. But these weren't things a teenager spends much time thinking about, so the anger and resentment that welled from these events began to spill into other parts of my life. The stockpile was building but it would take many years to burst into flames.

As my home life suffered, I focused more and more on my footy. I had moved from Robina High halfway through Year 10 to the well-known footy school of Palm Beach Currumbin High (PBC). PBC was one of a few schools around Queensland that offered rugby league pathways for students, combining traditional subjects with a focus on footy skills and strength. My future Broncos teammate Ben Hannant had been at the school a few years before me, following the likes of Ben Ikin from PBC into Queensland State of Origin jerseys. I switched to PBC hoping that it would help my rugby league develop. I was playing well with the Burleigh Bears, earning selection in the South Coast representative team every year for the state titles, but I still couldn't crack the Queensland team. I was starting to attract some attention from NRL clubs after playing well in the Burleigh Under 18 team. Former premiership winner Royce Simmons approached me on behalf of the Wests Tigers to discuss a scholarship with the team. Royce offered me $500 and told me that I would need to switch to the Tigers' preferred school of Keebra Park High for 2005. He even hooked up a phone call with Tigers coach Tim Sheens, who talked me through the opportunities that awaited me at the Tigers.

This was a big moment for me. I still hadn't made a Queensland team but the Tigers saw enough in me to make an offer – $500 was a lot for me back then. Despite this, the move to Keebra Park wasn't tempting. I enjoyed PBC and my classmates there, including Steve Michaels, and I was happy living with Nana. I didn't want to risk changing everything and heading to a new school. I politely declined the Tigers' offer. I returned to PBC for Year 12 determined to keep focusing on my footy and to improve as much as I could in my last year of school.

It is around this age when quite a few good young footy players often start to become more interested in other things in life. I was fortunate that those things didn't interest me too much. I hated the taste of beer and I didn't enjoy many other alcoholic drinks. I had a girlfriend but I was never too serious with my relationships at that age. And I didn't have much money to spend, so I wasn't able to go out many places. Footy was my natural haven from anything in the world that was troubling me, including the ongoing issues with Mum who continued to struggle with her mental health.

Other NRL teams began to take an interest in me. The Bulldogs offered me a two-year contract for $35 000 in total. That blew me away – I still hadn't made a Queensland representative team but I was being asked to become a professional rugby league player. All I had to do was sign the contract on the table in front of me. To this day, I'm not sure why I didn't jump at it immediately. It wasn't because of the money – $35 000 sounded like millions to me. I had told Nana at age eight that I wanted to be a professional rugby league player and here was the offer waiting for me to take it. But I wasn't a worldly kid. I liked living on the Gold Coast with Nana and I wasn't ready to live in Sydney. I'd never been there before. To be honest, the thought of moving to Sydney away from the only family that I knew terrified me. But my indecision paid off. Brisbane scouting legend Cyril Connell had approached my PBC school footy coach Rod Patison armed with a $1000 scholarship. Cyril told Rod it was the last scholarship he had for 2005, and asked which PBC player should get it. Cyril had suggested to Rod that he thought I had promise and Rod agreed. Thanks to them, my life changed forever.

Rod had done more for me than I could ever repay. It was more than teachers are supposed to do for their students. When I was struggling to get public transport to school, Rod organised for different teachers to give me lifts. He sat with me to interview prospective career managers and he provided advice when NRL clubs were interested in signing me. There was no incentive in this for Rod other than the satisfaction of helping a young kid. His was a kindness that I needed at a time when I wasn't sure how the world worked.

By signing with the Broncos, I had effectively traded the Bulldogs' $35 000 offer for a few pairs of footy boots and some shirts and shorts. Doesn't sound like a good business decision. But the Broncos were the team of my childhood and Brisbane was only a short drive from the Gold Coast. The letter from the Broncos' managing director Bruno Cullen spelled out the details of my deal with the Broncos:

It is our intention to offer Darius a scholarship from the beginning of 2005. The terms of the scholarship will be:

$500 for education purposes; $500 for rugby league
expenses which could include training gear, football
apparel, representative team selection, gym fees or other
incidental expenses. The Broncos place great importance
on a player's attitude as well as his ability to play rugby
league. To this end, the school principal will be contacted
regarding Darius' attitude and general behaviour at
school. It is a condition of this offer that the report is a
favourable one.

That wasn't a problem for me. I enjoyed school and didn't
bring much attention to myself. The scholarship helped me
get an invitation to a Broncos' young players' camp at their
Red Hill training base during the school holidays. I remember
Darren Lockyer speaking to us at the camp. I soaked up
every word he said when describing what it took to be a
professional footy player. I was so starstruck that I asked
him for an autograph. We then did some fitness work and
training drills to get a taste of everyday life for a professional
footballer. After the camp, the Broncos offered me a $20 000
contract for 2006, with NRL match payments on top of that.
I didn't expect to play a game so I didn't worry about match
payments. This was an offer that I couldn't pass up, even
though doubts soon began creeping in.

The Gold Coast Titans had been announced as a new team
for 2007. That sounded appealing to me – I could continue to
live with Nana and play on the Gold Coast. I rationalised that
if I had been offered a contract for the Broncos, then surely

I could get a deal as a local junior from the Titans? That's the state of mind I was in – the move to Brisbane was still scary even though I wouldn't be far from Nana. Despite these nagging doubts, I knew joining Brisbane would provide the chance to watch legends like Darren Lockyer at close hand and learn from coach Wayne Bennett. I came to realise this was the best option, so I signed my first professional football contract. Darius Boyd would become a Brisbane Bronco. Boy, that sounded weird.

The next few months were a blast. I made the Queensland Schoolboys team for the first time, and it was a decent team, too. We headed to Wagga Wagga for the national titles with a squad that included Israel Folau, Dave Taylor, Joel Moon and Esi Tonga who would all go on to play NRL. Then I was selected for the Australian team, which featured Akuila Uate, Michael Jennings, Mitch Pearce, Jarrod Mullen, Eddy Pettybourne and Mitch Aubusson. The Australian Schoolboys played the New Zealand Schoolboys in two international matches – one at Kougari Oval on Brisbane's bayside, and the other in Melbourne as a curtain-raiser for a Storm NRL match. I sometimes look back and think about the different paths that some of us took as schoolboy players. There were far better players than me at school who never cracked the NRL, and there were players who never got a look-in for junior representative teams who went on to become ten-year NRL players. When the NRL had an Under 20 competition, the conversion rate of its players to the NRL was about 10 per cent at best. And, if a player was one of the lucky ones to reach the NRL, he could look forward to an average NRL career of something like forty-four games. I've thought long and hard about the reasons why some players make it and others don't. It comes down to a combination of things: talent, body shape, professionalism, work ethic and a stack of luck.

I have my mum and my dad (who knows?) to thank for my body shape and talent, and my own narrow focus at that age helped my professionalism and work ethic. Thinking about footy and practising my skills distracted me from the general pain in other parts of my life. This fool's paradise was helping me greatly at that stage of my career; what I didn't know was that payback would eventually catch up to me. I had already had early luck – not signing with the Tigers or the Bulldogs and having my school coach recommend me for a $1000 Broncos scholarship. And I was lucky enough to avoid injury at that point in my career when some of my mates were starting to have problems. Also in my favour was that I wasn't a big party guy. That just didn't interest me. So I had at least a few things going for me in my hope to play NRL.

Despite this, I had never played a game of senior footy, so there was a long journey ahead. I was playing well for the Burleigh Bears colts team without pressing for a spot in their Queensland Cup side, but then I got lucky again. Burleigh's Trent Leis unfortunately suffered a minor injury and was unavailable for the Queensland Cup preliminary final against Redcliffe. I was called into the backline; my first senior footy game had arrived. Rick Stone, who would become an NRL coach in Newcastle, was in charge of Burleigh for my first game. I remember Rick being kind to me as I tried to get my head around making my debut in a semifinal against a Redcliffe team that was always strong. At least I was playing at home at Pizzey Park, where I had enjoyed a few good years. Burleigh won 24–19 and I was relieved that I made it through the game without making any glaring mistakes – which had been my main aim. Trent recovered to take his place in the Burleigh team that went down to the North Queensland Young Guns in the grand final.

The pace of my first senior game was faster than anything I had experienced. And the pace of the following weeks was frenetic as I finished Year 12 and prepared to join the Brisbane Broncos as a professional footballer. Before then, I had two days at the schoolies ritual in Surfers Paradise, which was straightforward for someone as boring as me. I went back to Nana's house and packed my bags for my new life in footy. On the day I left, Nana drove me to the train station where I nervously boarded a service for Brisbane, not having a clue what the next twelve months would hold.

UNCERTAINTY
2006–2010

CHAPTER 3

Welcome to the NRL

THE BRISBANE BRONCOS WERE THE BIGGEST SPORTING TEAM in town. Broncos fans would tell you they were one of the biggest brands in Australian sport. The club began in 1988 – only a few months after I was born – and they established a reputation for success. They won premierships in 1992 and 1993 and then claimed the only Super League championship ever played when rugby league split in 1997. You either dearly loved the Broncos or you deeply hated them. If you lived in New South Wales, you almost certainly hated them. There seemed to be no in-between. For some, the hatred only got deeper when Brisbane joined the re-unified league in 1998 and won the premiership. The Broncos won again in 2000, with me as a young teenager following every game I could. I would lie in front of the television at home with Mum to watch the

Broncos steam towards another premiership. That was the Broncos' fifth premiership in nine seasons. If they weren't the biggest brand in Australian sport, they were certainly the most successful modern-day club.

There were several familiar faces across that incredible winning run. The players whose names were well known even in Australian Rules states – Allan 'Alfie' Langer, Kevin Walters, Shane Webcke, Darren Lockyer, Brad Thorn, Steve Renouf, Wendell Sailor and Gorden Tallis. I had cheered all of them from the grandstands on those few times that Mum took me to Broncos games. I would practise Alfie's jinking runs and chip kicks. I would pretend I was Wendell charging down the touchline for another try. And I admired the smarts of Locky, who seemed to have all the time in the world to make split-second decisions. The Broncos had a mixture of tough, skilful forwards and backs who could blow teams away with speed, power and guile.

And there was Wayne Bennett – the 'Super Coach' as he was known. Wayne had been the Broncos' first coach and he was still in charge as I sat on a train heading to Roma Street Station to begin my time with the club. I had never spoken to Wayne and only knew the personality traits and details that most knew of him in the public realm: an inspirational bloke; a man of few words; a former police officer; a wise head and someone who developed quiet young footy players into people who could find their way in the world. By that stage, Wayne's coaching record included five premierships with the Broncos, multiple State of Origin series and ten Tests with Australia.

But, as I sat on that train heading for Brisbane, the Broncos weren't in a great place. They had fallen apart at the end of the 2005 season with seven straight losses. Two of those were in the finals series. This was new ground for Broncos fans. After the success of the previous decade, they were not used to a collapse like that, particularly in finals footy. Wayne had responded by parting ways with some of his coaching staff – Kevin Walters, Glenn Lazarus and Gary Belcher. That was a big story for Brisbane's rugby league media. Wayne had won premierships with Kevin and Glenn. He had coached Gary at Canberra in 1987 and in State of Origin. This was a major decision for Broncos fans not used to losing streaks or experiencing a breakdown in trusted relationships. But the end-of-season meltdown wasn't a surprise to some footy fans.

Earlier in the year, the Broncos had suffered a record 50–4 loss to the Melbourne Storm. It was the first time the Broncos had conceded 50 points. The Storm ran in ten tries and the Broncos' sole try came from Locky swooping on a pass from Melbourne fullback Billy Slater. The loss took the wind out of Broncos fans who had a false dawn of ten consecutive wins before the crash. These were tough times at the Broncos. What a time for a young bloke to be joining, especially someone like me already feeling homesick as the train pulled into Roma Street Station.

I didn't have long to miss everything I liked about the Gold Coast. I was met at the station by Paul Bunn, a generous man who was a key part of the Broncos' set-up. Paul was known for his scouting – he had signed Justin Hodges for the Broncos for $500 before he went on to become a frontline player in State of Origin football. Paul, his wife, Donna, and their fourteen-year-old twin boys were about to become my new Broncos 'family'. I would live in a home nicknamed 'Broncos House' with the Bunns, Joel Moon, John Te Reo, Dave Taylor and Sam Thaiday. Sammy had officially left Broncos House for his own place but he loved to come back and eat a decent meal there every few days. That was a good sign for me. The young players lived on the bottom level of the three-storey house. We had a ping-pong table, a swimming pool and a TV room. At first impression, it seemed very comfortable and I knew that I would be happy there.

I only had one night at Broncos House before my first adventure as a professional footballer began. The Broncos were heading off on a pre-season camp, where I would have the chance to meet my new teammates. I packed my swimming gear for the camp on the Sunshine Coast. We could take surfboards and anything else needed for a few days at the beach. What a start to my new job. The life of a professional footy player was sounding promising right from the start. That was until I arrived at the Broncos' training ground to find thirty bags in army camouflage colours lined up. They didn't look like the kind of bags you would take to the beach. We worked out quickly that we weren't going to the Sunshine Coast. We were heading for an army boot camp for six days. There would be no communication with anyone outside the playing group during that time. And there was no time to ring family members to tell them we wouldn't be in touch. The club took care of that.

I knew few of my teammates but I knew their names from watching them on television – some for at least a decade. Shane Webcke, Brad Thorn, Tonie Carroll and Petero Civoniceva were there. Locky had been allowed to miss the camp after a long season of club and representative games. Wayne Bennett came along as did my old mate Steve Michaels, who was one familiar face from childhood. I remember Justin Hodges being there simply because I can recall how much he hated it. I wasn't sure how to feel – I was excited and felt like asking for the autographs of some of my new teammates but I was also trying hard not to miss home. My classmates were still on schoolies week as I boarded a bus for the unknown.

My memory of those six days is crystal clear. I remember the food rations that helped to drop my weight from ninety to eighty-five kilograms during the trip. I remember an abseiling exercise that terrified the boys who hated heights. My old teammate Greg Eastwood was one of those, refusing to participate in the cliff descent. That was until the boot camp leader tempted Greg with a promise – if he completed the abseiling exercise then we would all eat chicken for dinner that night. I can't tell you how exciting that was to a big group of hungry blokes. It was enough to convince Greg to conquer his fears and abseil down the cliff face, to our unbridled relief. We had chicken for dinner that night, although it wasn't as we had expected. Two live chickens were let loose in our camping area. They were our dinner for the night. We had to catch them, pluck them and cook them up. Two chickens for thirty starving humans. I can honestly say that I have never had a worse chicken meal in my life. It was gluey and tasteless and pushed us further out of our comfort zones, which had already been left a long way behind. The meal marked the end of a bad day, although it was a worse day if you were the chickens.

Early on I learnt that my new teammate Brad Thorn – who would later switch to rugby union and play for the All Blacks – was a caring guy; although he didn't make much of a medical specialist. On one of the first few days in the camp, I felt something weird under my arm and as I couldn't quite see it, I asked Brad for his appraisal. 'That's nothing mate, just a mole,' Brad confidently told me in his evenly paced, quiet way. I didn't remember having a mole there but Brad could see it better than I could. Two days later, it eventuated that the 'mole' was actually a tick, which had to be carefully removed. Schoolies was starting to look a whole lot better. But everything was temporarily forgotten when, on the last night, we were served up about two hundred pieces of fried chicken. I remember everything about that chicken – its taste, its feel and the juices running down my hands. That remains one of the greatest meals I have ever had.

We returned to Brisbane and I began trying to regain the five kilograms I had lost during boot camp. I needed the weight because I didn't have much muscle at that age and I knew I would probably be playing men for the first time with a full season looming in the Queensland Cup for the Broncos' feeder club, the Toowoomba Clydesdales. Training hard had never been a problem for me so I steadily regained weight and I handled my first pre-season well. To be honest, I had been scared of the NRL pre-season since the Broncos were candid with us on the mid-year camp I attended with other scholarship holders a few months earlier. They told us that pre-seasons were the worst time of the year, when you did nothing but exercise that pushed you to vomiting point. Their warning frightened me into training extra hard while I was still at school to ensure that I wouldn't be at the back of the pack in pre-season. The fact that I held my own boosted my confidence.

I would return on the train every weekend to stay with Nana in her townhouse. It was always great to see her because I was still missing her and my old life. She offered me her wisdom at a time when it felt like I was living a surreal life training with the footy team I grew up supporting. Nana was seventy-six at that stage and was finding it hard to do some of the things that had come easier to her a few years earlier. She was also starting to struggle with my mum, who remained in a mental health facility. Nana had always remained positive about Mum, even when I began to have difficulty accepting the situation. Nana would remind me of Mum's good points as my teenage mind struggled to deal with her life away from me.

At that age, I felt that Mum had abandoned me. For a few years she had been moving between hospital wards and mental health facilities. I was confused because I couldn't understand the depth of her mental health issues. I knew Mum wasn't physically ill, so why had she not been able to look after me? She kept telling me that she was dying but there was nothing physically wrong, so how could that be? Looking back now, I recognise that we have come so far in our understanding of mental health challenges, but I didn't know much back then. At the time, I had a meeting with a psychologist arranged by the mental health facility that Mum was staying in, but my mind was too closed at that point, so the session wasn't useful.

Nana was also beginning to find it difficult to deal with Mum's mental health and her frustration started to show. Nana was from an era in which mental health problems weren't spoken about. And they weren't understood. Eventually, Nana's frustration in finding herself as a woman in her seventies trying to raise a teenager – and not being able to do many things like drive at night – boiled over. Nana and Mum had a falling-out and that did nothing to improve my relationship with Mum. Nana was very dear to me and the pain she felt only reinforced my decision to effectively cut Mum out of my life for the time being. Nana didn't want that, but it was confusing for all of us as we tried to cope with the fact that we were unable to help Mum.

Football remained my great distraction and I finally arrived at my first pre-season game for the Broncos. I was part of a very young Broncos team to play a very young North Queensland Cowboys team in Rockhampton. Most of the senior players from both teams were rested for this game as the Broncos and Cowboys took the chance to look at a few young players like me. We still had Karmichael Hunt in the halves and Dane Carlaw in the forward pack but these teams would look very different from those that would meet a few weeks later in the opening match of the NRL season at Suncorp Stadium. I was rapt to play a game for the Broncos and I was even more excited to wear the No. 1 jersey – my favourite position growing up. I thought it would be one of the few times that I would wear a Broncos jersey that year because I expected to play a full season for the Toowoomba Clydesdales. I had a decent game that night and I remember the excitement of wearing that jersey. I gave it to Nana to thank her for all she had done for me, and I still have it today.

The second pre-season game was in the New South Wales town of Port Macquarie against the Canberra Raiders. I remember it clearly because I was part of the Broncos squad that went to an autograph session in Port Macquarie. I hadn't done one before – the players sat at long tables as fans walked along with Broncos posters for us to sign. I was sitting in between Tonie Carroll, who had been playing State of Origin for eight years, and Leon Bott, who had played on the wing in every game for the Broncos in 2005. Some fans walked along to get Tonie's autograph before moving along the line to where I sat with my pen at the ready, only to pull back their poster and take it to Leon, leaving me sitting there. I can't blame them – I was an eighteen-year-old who had never been near an NRL field, so they probably thought I was the ball boy. And I did nothing in the game that followed to convince them otherwise. It was my first game of NRL standard – the Broncos and Raiders ran out strong teams that night – and I didn't play well. I was hit in one tackle that winded me and jolted the ball free for a knock-on. It was the first time I had been hit in a good tackle from an NRL player and I felt it immediately. On the bus on the way home I felt disappointed, realising that I had locked in my season playing in the Queensland Cup. We had some injuries in the backline, including State of Origin centre Brent Tate, but even with the chance of some places opening up, it was unlikely I'd be asked to play.

I wasn't in the team for our final pre-season game – a clash with the Melbourne Storm in Toowoomba. This was the rehearsal for our opening NRL match and Wayne Bennett had picked his strongest side. That didn't surprise me and I wasn't disappointed because I had not expected to play in the NRL that year. On the day before the game in Toowoomba, Wayne told me that Justin Hodges had an injury and wouldn't play. He was going to be marking Greg Inglis that night in Toowoomba. Greg was the next big thing in footy at that stage. He had been stunning for the Norths Devils in the Queensland Cup, earning a call-up to the Storm for his debut during the 2005 season. The Broncos were all too familiar with Greg because he had been on the field only a few minutes in the 2005 qualifying final at Suncorp Stadium when he scored the match-winning try without a hand being laid on him. I had played against Greg a few times in schoolboy matches, so Wayne asked if I wanted to mark him in the pre-season match. I wasn't going to knock that back so I played and thankfully was much better than the previous week. At the very least, I didn't let anyone down so that was a good thing.

A strange thing happened at training the following week. I started training in the top team, standing on the left wing outside Shaun Berrigan. There were two weeks left until the first game so I thought this may be a good sign for me. But I fully expected that Wayne would change things around and I would go back to training with the reserves team. He didn't and I started thinking I was a chance to play in the season opener despite only having played one competition game of senior footy. We weren't stocked with representative wingers that year so I was in the right position. I knew I was fit and performing well in the pre-season drills, so that was also positive. I was a competitor in anything that I did and I put safety ahead of being flashy on the field. Wayne liked all those things so I guess they helped me win selection on the left wing when the team for the first game was named.

I was shocked. I texted some of my mates to tell them and I rang Nana, who couldn't believe it. The Broncos were really good to Nana. They organised for her to come to the game in a limousine, picking her up from her townhouse on the Gold Coast and bringing her to Suncorp Stadium for our Sunday afternoon game. That was a huge thrill for her. She was in as much disbelief at my selection as I was. Neither of us had expected this when Nana had driven me to the train station four months earlier for my move to Brisbane.

I had nothing to say in the change rooms before the game. I was edgy but the nerves weren't suffocating – they were a mixture of excitement and butterflies. Everything was new to me at Suncorp Stadium, but many of my teammates knew this ground well. It was another day at the office for the likes of Shane Webcke and Brad Thorn, who went about their careful routines to get ready to play. I took a peek at Darren Lockyer but that probably wasn't wise because I don't think Locky has looked nervous at any time in his life. As we prepared to run out on to Suncorp Stadium, there were more than one thousand combined games' experience in our team. Not one of those came from me.

I will never forget the noise of the Broncos supporters as I ran on to the ground that day. It was deafening. Months of frustration at the seven-match losing streak exploded as we ran on to our home ground before almost 50000 people on that sticky Sunday afternoon. I'm not sure how many of those 50000 knew anything about me but that was fine with me – I was happy to be as anonymous as possible. I wasn't playing football because I wanted people to know about me. I was playing because I loved playing rugby league. If I could do that and stay anonymous, that would be perfect. But it didn't take me long to learn that my days of anonymity were over. As I took a step on to that famous ground, my life began to change forever.

CHAPTER 4

Joining Dad's Army

WAYNE BENNETT AND THE BRISBANE BRONCOS WERE A combination that dated back to my birth. When I came along in July 1987, the Broncos and Wayne were settling on his deal to be the club's foundation coach. Wayne signed with the Broncos while he was in Canberra in the first season of a four-year deal with the Raiders. He was persuaded to return home by his old mate Paul 'Porky' Morgan, one of the Broncos' founders and a former teammate of Wayne's. The Broncos had just been given a licence to join the then New South Wales Rugby League and they only wanted Wayne as coach. The story goes that Porky went to Canberra and refused to leave until Wayne found a way out of his Raiders deal. I reckon Wayne would have driven a hard bargain – he's a master negotiator – but the deal was worth it because it started one of the most successful coaching stints in modern Australian sporting history. Wayne was entering his nineteenth season in charge when I arrived at the club, and the Broncos had not missed the finals since 1991. Even a teenager like me without much knowledge of how the world worked knew Wayne Bennett was a big deal in rugby league.

I knew of his reputation but I didn't know a thing about Wayne as a person. I had seen him in the flesh only once before when he ran a coaching clinic at PBC high school. I didn't talk to him there and, to be honest, I didn't talk to him a whole lot through 2006. As it turned out, I realised Wayne and I had a lot in common – we don't say too much and we like to sit back and observe before we talk. I learnt a lot about Wayne from watching him as a coach, especially the way that he connected with everyone in the team, from the outgoing to the introverted and from senior players to the rookies like me. He has used that ability to his tremendous advantage throughout his coaching career. Wayne was a police officer in his younger days, while he was also playing rugby league for Queensland and Australia, and I reckon he would have been a calming influence among a hostile crowd. He faced some tough moments in the police force so life in the footy world wasn't so difficult.

Wayne was old-fashioned in some respects. He wanted us to dress appropriately – he didn't like hats, singlets or thongs, particularly at the dinner table. He also didn't think much of flashy hairstyles – a short back and sides was fine by Wayne. One thing that surprised me watching Wayne in my early months was his ability to motivate players in different ways – and that included raising his voice when needed. I didn't expect that because Wayne had always seemed so calm in interviews I had seen, even when his team had lost and he probably had every right to become annoyed. I expected he would be the same in his daily coaching style but I noticed that he would sometimes get frustrated with certain players during training and give them a decent spray. I feared the same treatment if I didn't train well, but then I worked out that Wayne knew the players who needed a rev-up and those who didn't. I was a perfectionist so I didn't need someone shouting at me when I made a mistake. I would play the mistake over in my mind dozens of times so an extra voice wasn't helpful. Wayne quickly worked out that I needed encouragement, not criticism, when I made an error, which was (and still is) one of his many skills as a coach.

There was one place, however, that I couldn't escape Wayne's criticism – the Monday 'tip sheet' that summed up the previous weekend's game. This became my new version of hell in my first season at the Broncos. I was already feeling intimidated as the rookie in a team of rugby league superstars, keeping my head down and trying not to draw attention to myself. And then I found out that, every Monday after a game, Wayne would distribute a sheet to the team that listed every player's statistics from the game, a comment from the coach and a mark out of ten for how they had played. I was petrified. I imagined Darren Lockyer with a bunch of great stats, a rating of nine out of ten and a comment from Wayne along the lines of: 'Another great game from a super player.' Same for Shane Webcke, Justin Hodges, Petero Civoniceva and the rest. As for me? All I could imagine was a handful of stats, a very modest rating and a comment that I had a lot to learn.

Halfway through our opening match against the North Queensland Cowboys, no one was in line for a good tip sheet the next day. The Broncos were trailing 0–24 at half-time and we were lucky not to trail by more as Matt Bowen and Johnathan Thurston carved us up. We started the game badly and we kept going that way. I knew things weren't going well for us early because Locky gave the referee some direct advice and copped a penalty for dissent. I had seen enough of Locky's games on television to know that this was very unlike him. I was probably the only Broncos player not feeling downcast at half-time because everything was new to me. I was dealing with the novelty of a crowd of almost 50 000 which drowned out anything my teammates said to me. I was stargazing up close at the Cowboys team that was filled with players who had competed in the grand final only a few months earlier and who I'd been watching on television for years. And I was enjoying the challenge of marking Matt Sing, who had played in Queensland's Origin team for the last eleven seasons. In the end, we lost 36–4 with the only try coming to me in the left corner. I was excited to get a try in my first game but I kept that hidden because no Broncos supporter in that ground was ready to celebrate. The scoreboard looked brutal so I planted the ball, turned around and went back to my position for the restart.

They say that you learn more in defeat than victory and that was the case throughout the 2006 season. The media began to kick us around because we had just lost our eighth consecutive match stretching back to the collapse at the end of 2005. They called us 'Dad's Army' in reference to the older players in our team. I heard this from some teammates and from Nana, because I had made a decision not to read, watch or listen to any media reports during the season. Wayne told us to ignore them because they wouldn't help our games, particularly for young players like me. I followed Wayne's advice – I didn't need the distraction. Wayne told us that if we absolutely had to read sports reports, then we should wait until after a game finished to read stories from the previous week.

During the tough week that followed the Cowboys loss, our older players didn't flinch. If they had read the papers, they were using them as motivation rather than as a distraction. Our forwards were an older, hard-headed group. The likes of Shane Webcke, Brad Thorn, Petero Civoniceva and Tonie Carroll worked very hard but they didn't seem to say much, especially to me. They led by example and didn't care for anything flashy. You had to earn their respect and trust. I liked that about the Broncos culture because I didn't want to let anyone down. I didn't talk much with the forwards because we would train in our own groups – the forwards, halves and hookers, and outside backs were separated – before coming together for team runs. I enjoyed our outside backs group, which included the likes of Karmichael Hunt, Justin Hodges, Brent Tate, Shaun Berrigan and my old mate Steve Michaels.

This was a good group for me. We were a bit younger than the forwards and we got on quite well. I will always be grateful to Hodgo and Karmichael for looking out for me that season and making me feel welcomed.

Looking back, there were plenty of reasons to think that the Broncos' 2006 season was going to be challenging: Wayne had overhauled his coaching staff by parting ways with some much-loved former Broncos; people were still debating whether Locky was a five-eighth or whether he should return to fullback; Wayne had spoken about changing our playing style to play wider rather than down the middle with our big forwards; some of our best players were in their twilight years; and we had lost six consecutive finals matches including two in the last year. We had become known for late-season fade-outs so, with all of this happening and the grim start against the Cowboys, there were valid reasons for fans to think that this would be another tough year.

But we found our way in Round 2 when we travelled to Shark Park and knocked off Cronulla 16–12. It was my first win as an NRL player but it was sweeter for my teammates who had lived through the eight-game losing streak. We came back to Suncorp Stadium and scored 30 points for the first time since Round 14, 2005, when we easily beat the Parramatta Eels. We thrashed the Roosters in Sydney on Good Friday night, which began to silence our critics, before we returned home and defeated Canberra to establish a 6–2 win–loss record after eight rounds. I had played in each game and hadn't let the team down. This NRL thing wasn't too bad.

Off the field, I was trying to adjust to my new life as a professional footballer. My contract included a base payment throughout the year of $20 000 followed by match payments of $2000. That sounded like a good deal for the Broncos because I didn't expect to play in the NRL. But, after eight rounds, I had $16 000 in match payments sitting in my bank account. This was huge money for an eighteen-year-old who had been used to making do with $70 pay cheques from helping to run coaching clinics on the Gold Coast. I didn't know what to do with the money, so I didn't do anything. My base pay was covering my expenses, which were $150 a week for board at Broncos House, and the usual things like a car, fuel, phone bill and some clothes. I had bought a car with the help of the Broncos because I really had no idea how to do that. That was another great strength of Wayne as a coach – he would make sure we learnt how to do things properly away from footy. He wanted us to learn about life as well as footy so he would make sure we had access to people who could teach us the basics of adult living. Given my struggles at home in recent years, I found Wayne's help in this part of my life invaluable.

The footy season rolled into the representative season, which seriously damaged our Broncos team. Three Broncos were chosen for the Australian team to play in the Anzac Test while eight Broncos were chosen for Queensland in the State of Origin series. That left a massive hole in our club team so we had to dig deep for replacement players. Karmichael Hunt was in the Test and Origin team so I replaced him at fullback for a match against the Knights in Newcastle. Knights legend Andrew 'Joey' Johns played in the Anzac Test earlier that weekend – it was his last game of representative football – but he backed up two days later for his beloved Knights. I was warned about Joey's spiral bombs, which were a nightmare for experienced fullbacks let alone eighteen-year-olds who had only watched him play on television. The spiral bombs speared off his foot, twisted endlessly and dipped and dived in ways that were different each time. When you had a few defenders storming through, Joey's spiral bombs were apparently not much fun. Wayne expected that Joey would target me so he asked Locky, before his Test commitments, to hit me with a barrage of spiral bombs at training. It wasn't a bad way to get ready for the game – instead of Joey I had Locky kicking at me and he knew how to launch spiral bombs. I felt well prepared after working with Locky, but I still wasn't looking forward to standing in front of a huge Newcastle crowd while their favourite player tried to make me into a circus act. Funnily enough, after all that preparation, Joey didn't kick a spiral bomb all day. Not one. I wasn't sure whether to be annoyed, because I'd done so much practice, or relieved that I didn't have to contend with the kicks. We lost that game 32–30, with Joey kicking a penalty goal to get the Knights home.

I had made it through twelve rounds in the NRL without too many problems but the game was about to give me the first of several reality checks. Rounds 13 and 14 were two that I'd rather forget – although a concussion in Round 14 meant I had no trouble forgetting that one. Round 13 included my first trip to New Zealand to play the Warriors in Auckland. As I sat in the change rooms before the game, I realised I wasn't looking forward to playing. That was new to me – I always loved playing rugby league. You name the time and the venue and I would be there five minutes early. But that day I was unsettled as we prepared to take on a Warriors team with the biggest backline I had ever encountered. And they were all fast. I had a taste of the power and speed of a Polynesian backline when I had played the Junior Kiwis the previous year. The Warriors were a much larger version of the Junior Kiwis and they included Manu Vatuvei, a hulking winger who had twenty kilograms on me. I knew the Warriors would be coming at me at full speed. My uncharacteristic nerves before the game impacted my performance. I remember halfback Grant Rovelli, another Queenslander in his first year in the league, coming to tackle me. I tried to palm him off but Grant belted me over the sideline. A photo of me being upended was published in the next day's paper. Nana cut out every picture and mention of me in the newspapers and kept them in a scrapbook. Even the time when a halfback speared me over the touchline.

We won that game against the Warriors, but without much of a contribution from me. To be blunt, I was ordinary in that game. As we flew back home, I was already fearing the Monday tip sheet with Wayne's observations of the game. I was right to be worried. When Wayne handed out the tip sheet the next day, I felt like disappearing into the change-room lockers at our Red Hill base. The tip sheet had me

57

labelled for the passenger I was in that game. Wayne gave me a mark of three out of ten and he followed up with a comment that I still remember, word for word: 'Didn't deserve to shower with the boys.' Ouch. That hurt. But that's what happens when you have only seven involvements – five runs and two tackles – in eighty minutes. I was mortified, especially considering what the likes of Locky, Shane and Petero might have thought about that.

Eight of our Origin players were missing for the Round 14 match at Sydney's Olympic Stadium when we took on South Sydney Rabbitohs, who hadn't won a game that season. The Bunnies weren't flash in 2006 but they sensed they had a chance against a Broncos team minus all of our big names. The team changes meant that the whole cast of Broncos House, where I had been living for the last seven months, would play together for the first time. Dave Taylor, the schoolboy with the freakish skills, made his debut that night. My Queensland and Australian Schoolboys mate Joel Moon also played. We were a bunch of kids taking on a team that was desperate to win on a wet and cold night in Sydney. I played fullback and held my own until Souths veteran Adam MacDougall elbowed me in the head and knocked me out cold. That was the first concussion of my career. I don't remember a thing about it but I remember Nana's reaction. She had MacDougall marked on her villains' list forever because he elbowed me and then stood over me roaring as I saw stars on the ground. That didn't sit well with her, and she left that incident out of her scrapbook. My NRL learning curve was continuing.

The Broncos' main goal that winter was to finish the State of Origin period sitting as close to the top of the table as we could. It was weird to be playing with so many stars of the game one week and then to have so many inexperienced players, including me, around the next week. At one stage that season we had to call on Nick Emmett at the last minute after a player was injured. Nick was playing in the Queensland Cup for Redcliffe and had never met our acting captain Shane Webcke, who had retired from representative footy. Nick introduced himself to Shane in the change rooms before the game. We had all of our players back for a Round 16 match against the Manly Sea Eagles at Brookvale Oval – this game fell between the second and third Origin games. I was at fullback again as Karmichael Hunt was injured. It was a tough game, highlighted by Brent Tate's superb individual try when he scorched sixty metres to quieten the Brookvale crowd for a few seconds. I remember the game for another reason – the tension was high in the final minutes when the Sea Eagles were peppering me with bombs. I took one kick a couple of minutes before full-time, which had been swirling around with the help of the Manly sea breeze. We won the game and went to Sydney Airport to catch a flight home. At the airport, I ducked into the toilet for a quick stop before jumping on the plane. I was standing at the urinal when Wayne walked in and used the urinal next to me. As we were going about our business in silence, he piped up: 'You did well to catch that kick at the end. Well done.' That was it – praise Wayne Bennett–style, delivered at the urinal at Sydney Airport. It seems funny looking back at it but the location didn't matter – the praise meant a lot to me in that first year.

The Broncos got through the Origin period relatively well – Locky went out of his way to thank the young guys for their efforts – and then we prepared for the run to the finals. That's when the trouble started, with five straight losses. We lost to the Cowboys again and we fell twice to the Melbourne Storm in that period. The Storm were strong favourites to win the premiership and we were again under the pump from the media who were writing about another Broncos late-season collapse. Wayne was insistent that we weren't in a 'slump'. That's the word the media kept using but, after each of the five losses, Wayne insisted it wasn't a slump. Behind closed doors, he began to tinker with a few things in ways that would become familiar to me over the years. He called a meeting with all the players to tell us that it was time for us to make a sacrifice as a sign that we were prepared to do whatever it took to play good football. He demanded that we all make a sacrifice right there – what were we going to give up? Most of the players said they wouldn't touch any alcohol until the season finished. I didn't drink much alcohol so I said I would give up junk food. That was a sacrifice for me because I had just turned nineteen and had little idea how to look after my body, so fast food was an easy friend. It wasn't unusual for me and my mates to pass time by pulling up at a service station at 10 p.m. and wolfing down a chicken roll. I had a can of soft drink with dinner every night. I look back on that now with a smile, because as my career went on, I became so strict with what I consumed. The sacrifice worked because though I dearly missed those chicken rolls for the final months of the season, it served as a reminder that I was playing a level of football that required a change in attitude.

We began to turn things around in Round 23 when we lost to the Storm on a Sunday afternoon at Suncorp Stadium. We didn't lose by much and we showed plenty of bright moments against the team that sealed the minor premiership that day – though there were still three rounds until the finals. That's how far the Storm had kicked away from the rest of the field – there was no doubt that the Storm, under coach Craig Bellamy and captain Cameron Smith, were the premiership favourites. We then went to Sydney and thrashed the Bulldogs – a top four team at the time – 30–0. That was the performance that we had been looking for and missing those chicken rolls was starting to seem worthwhile. I had played in every game that season but I would miss the Round 25 game against the Eels at Parramatta Stadium. Wayne told me that I needed a weekend off because I had never played in a season of this length and at this standard. Then he left me with a challenge: he said I would play in the final regular season game against the Warriors at Suncorp Stadium, but then all bets were off. I had to prove that I was worthy of making the team for the finals. That got me worried because I figured Wayne would most likely be choosing between me and Tame Tupou, who had played Tests for New Zealand that year.

We thumped Parramatta 23–0 and then came home for the Warriors match. Wayne moved me to the right wing for the first time that season, outside Brent Tate who was playing very good footy. That left me marking Manu Vatuvei – the player I had been so nervous about only a few months earlier in Auckland. But it's funny how a few months and a few lessons can help build confidence. I was much more settled that day because I'd realised that players like Manu may have had twenty kilograms on me but our strengths and weaknesses didn't match up. I had my skills, fitness and footwork against the strength, speed and high-jumping ability of the likes of Manu. Once I changed my mindset, I became willing to back myself against players who were bigger and stronger than me. I played well in the Warriors game and I was chosen for the opening finals match against the St George Illawarra Dragons at Suncorp Stadium the following week.

Finals footy is a special time for fans, but I reckon few people love it as much as Wayne Bennett. The start of the 2006 finals series was my first glimpse into how Wayne changed at this time of year. He made sure that we knew that finals were a big deal by changing our routines and even changing the hotels we stayed at in Sydney. We really didn't have many plays or game plans during the regular season – we worked to a system that had been successful for Wayne for a long time. But during the finals, we suddenly had more plays and we had more of a focus on game plans. The 2006 finals carried an extra edge for Wayne because the Broncos had lost six finals straight. For all of the team's past success, achieving five premierships in nine years, the Broncos were under pressure as the media continued to remind everyone that we had a shocking record in recent finals. In addition, we then had a media distraction that seemed to lift Wayne to even greater heights – the league world was beside itself after a story broke claiming that Wayne had been set to sign with the Sydney Roosters until the deal fell over at the last moment. Talk about drama at finals time – Wayne probably didn't like the publicity from that story but he loved the edge that it provided our finals build-up.

The pressure tightened when our finals losing streak continued in the qualifying final held on a Saturday night at Suncorp Stadium. The Dragons brushed us off too easily in a 20–4 victory. We had made our intentions clear in the first set as our big guys trucked it up the middle – our first four plays were runs from Shane Webcke, Dane Carlaw, Petero Civoniceva and Sam Thaiday. They were great players to run off but the Dragons had the wood on the Broncos during that decade and we never troubled them that night. I scored our only try in the right corner when the game was already getting beyond us. That was deflating because it meant the rest of our matches would be on the road and against teams that were in form. But that's when Wayne began to go into overdrive – well, as much as Wayne can move at speed – to get our minds on track for our semifinal the following week against Newcastle at the Sydney Football Stadium.

Wayne had one advantage up his sleeve that he was about to utilise. With the finals in mind, he had begun making surprise changes to our play in a way that I still find hard to comprehend. It seems crazy that this happened so close to the end of the season – the finals were a week away when the switches began – but it worked. Some of our key players changed positions between attack and defence. Shaun Berrigan went from attacking at left centre to causing havoc for opposition defenders at dummy half. But he defended in the centres. That gave Berro plenty of energy in attack because poor Shane Perry had to defend in the hooker's role while attacking at halfback. Justin Hodges was in the centres in attack and at fullback in defence. David Stagg attacked on the left wing. We had to get our heads around those new positions quickly and since it was a struggle for us, it also caused problems for the opposition working out how to adjust their game plans.

Wayne's changes began to pay off when we played Newcastle. The Knights had rolled Manly in the first week of the finals and they had Andrew Johns running their show. I was marking Anthony Quinn that night but I didn't have much to do in defence. We thrashed the Knights, starting with a fifteenth-minute try to David Stagg in the left corner that was sparked by Locky's vision. Three minutes later, Locky passed to Karmichael Hunt whose flick pass found Brent Tate for a good try. Hodgo, playing in the centres in attack, collected a Locky grubber kick for a try fifteen minutes later and that match was as good as over. In the final minute before half-time, Berro sprinted around some tired middle defenders to set up a try, again showing that Wayne's positional changes were causing trouble for our opponents. When I scored a try in the fifty-sixth minute, taking the last of eleven passes in an awesome team movement, we led 50–0. A new hotel, new positions and the Broncos' first finals win after seven straight losses. Things were looking up.

We knew, however, that our next assignment would be tough – a preliminary final against the Bulldogs at the Sydney Football Stadium. The Bulldogs were still hurting from our 30–0 win over them five weeks earlier and they had returned to form, beating Canberra in the first week of the finals to go straight through to the grand final qualifier. They had their big bodies up front – Willie Mason being the best known of a 'Dogs pack desperate for revenge. And they looked good. We scored the first try after a few minutes but the Bulldogs then ran in 20 unanswered points including a fine try from a Mason flick pass to halfback Brent Sherwin. I wasn't going well – I was marking stocky winger Matt Utai who bulldozed over the top of me for a try. I also let a 40–20 kick go over my head at a crucial time, giving the Bulldogs a key possession. We went to half-time down 6–20 and the crowd was letting us have it as we went into the change rooms.

Then, the strangest thing happened as we headed up the tunnel for half-time. The teams were not far apart and as we walked we could hear the Bulldogs crowing. Willie Mason told his teammates: 'We're going to the grand final boys.' I didn't hear it but enough of my teammates did. Especially Petero Civoniceva and Brad Thorn. As we reached the rooms, our big men were fuming. They didn't need much help to get fired up, and Big Willie's words had flicked a switch in them. As usual, Wayne was calm; he didn't seem too worried about Willie's words, although he made sure the whole team knew about them. Wayne told us that the next forty minutes was the time for the true believers – it was the time when our work in pre-season, the demands of the army boot camp and the bonds created between teammates over many seasons would bring their rewards. And he reminded us that this was the perfect chance to silence the critics who thought the Broncos had become late-season fade-outs.

Those next forty minutes remain some of the most memorable in my career. Just four minutes into the half, we scored an incredible try when Hodgo fielded a Bulldogs kick in our in-goal and then started a 35-metre run before slipping a pass to Shaun Berrigan who brushed off defenders, changed the ball in his hand then stood on his head as Willie Mason tried to tackle him in the corner, reaching out to score a superhuman try. Four minutes after that, Dane Carlaw scored just centimetres from where Berro planted the ball. Eleven minutes after that, we went sixty metres and I was lucky enough to finish off a movement that featured plenty of our big names. We hit the front with that conversion. Six minutes later, Locky put on a vintage show, stepping his way past the Bulldogs, passing to Tonie Carroll and then backing up to score. When Brent Tate scored with ten minutes to go, again after a Locky stepping show, we were out of the Bulldogs' reach. To finish off, Locky added a field goal and Corey Parker scored in the corner. The Bulldogs were done and we were off to the grand final. With those forty minutes, we had buried our reputation for fading out and Wayne had overseen another miracle to annoy his critics.

As expected, Melbourne qualified for the grand final with a comfortable win over the Dragons, leaving us to face the Storm for the premiership. We were outsiders – no one could argue that – so we were in a position that Wayne loved. The next week was head-spinning. Fewer than twelve months earlier, I had been at school, hoping that I would be good enough to play a full season in the Queensland Cup for the Toowoomba Clydesdales. Never did I expect to play twenty-six out of a possible twenty-seven games leading into a grand final in Sydney. We had massive crowds at training each day before we left early for Sydney for the traditional grand final festivities.

Wayne was in his element all week. There was only one thing Wayne loved more than finals football – playing in a grand final. And a grand final against a red-hot favourite was perfect for him. He was on his toes all week, looking at ways he could motivate us for a game against a Storm team that had been building for a few years. I look back on that night as a clash of the established club and the NRL's new top team. The Broncos had our veteran players and then youngsters including Hodgo, Sam Thaiday, Corey Parker and me, who would play for another decade or so. The Storm had their old heads including Scott Hill and Matt Geyer, but they were about to surf a wave of young talent including captain Cameron Smith, Cooper Cronk, Billy Slater and Greg Inglis who all started in that grand final. It was set to be a great game and that's what we got in front of almost 80 000 people at the Olympic Stadium.

I was on the right wing, playing outside Brent Tate and marking Steve Turner. I didn't have to wait long for action as Scott Hill twisted, turned, dummied and drew me into a tackle, sending a pass around the corner for Steve to score. We hit back in the nineteenth minute when Locky skipped across the posts, drawing defenders before turning inside to Hodgo for a try. The premiership would be decided in the sixty-first minute with a try that summed up our season. We had a play-the-ball about forty metres out from the line when Berro found Locky, who made something out of nothing. Locky gave a quick pass to Corey Parker before an offload to Casey McGuire. That's when the movement looked dead until Casey threw the ball over his head to find Locky – who else? – backing up before he passed to Tonie Carroll who ran ten metres before the final pass to Brent Tate who completed the try inches from the sideline. That was our season – a great start, very wobbly middle, a promising burst but the likelihood that the ending would be rough. It wasn't.

I was running alongside Tatey the whole way and I was pumped as we edged to a 14–8 lead. The icing came with a Locky field goal in the seventy-third minute. It was fitting that the final two hit-ups to lay the platform for that field goal came from Shane Webcke and Brad Thorn. We celebrated a few minutes later as the final siren sounded, delivering a premiership that had not looked likely at many stages throughout the year. The next few days were a blur – a long night of celebrations, a fan day at the Broncos clubhouse the following day and a parade through the Queen Street Mall in Brisbane riding in convertible cars.

Nana seemed to be more excited than I was at the premiership win. She was as proud as I'd ever seen her, taking great care in her collection of newspaper articles and photos that she was building at home. She would even pause the television if I was on it and take a photo to show me. She was particularly proud when her long-time friends rang her to say how happy they were for her on the Broncos' win. Hearing Nana so happy gave me perhaps my greatest thrill of the year. I could never repay her so I was pleased for any time that I made her feel good.

That 2006 season taught me things that I would remember throughout my career. I learnt about the culture of respect and trust. I had found it hard to trust people during my life but that group of players gave me a valuable grounding in trust. They also demanded respect – they never asked for it but their actions made it clear that these teammates expected nothing less than full commitment and a promise to play for each other. And that all stemmed from Wayne, who quickly became an important part of my life. I felt that I could trust Wayne and that was extremely important to me at that age. He stood by me that year when there were plenty of times he could have picked someone else to play in my position. If he had dropped me, the papers would barely have mentioned it. But he gave a young kid a go without any certainty I would be up to the challenge. That meant a lot to me. I didn't want to let him down and I didn't want to let my teammates down. Those lessons would remain with me forever.

But there was one thing that I was still to learn – premierships were very hard to win. I didn't understand that as I rode in that convertible car through the Queen Street Mall waving at thousands of supporters. The previous ten months had been a haze of new teammates, new experiences and the great feeling of winning a grand final. It wouldn't take me long to learn that professional sport wasn't all tries and trophies.

CHAPTER 5

Wearing maroon

IN FEWER THAN TWELVE MONTHS, I HAD A PREMIERSHIP ring and memories for a lifetime. But I didn't have a washing machine. And that was a problem because my time at Broncos House was over and I was moving into a new phase of my life. Not long after the 2006 grand final, I said farewell to the Bunn family, who had been incredible in my first move out of home. The Bunns treated me like their own son and I loved that there were always people around that house. Coming from a small family, the noise and company of a full house was important to me as I coped with my new life playing professional football. I moved out with my old junior representative teammates Steve Michaels and Denan Kemp into a house that our teammate Dane Carlaw rented to us for the year. The house was perfect – we just didn't have anything to put in it. We washed our clothes at the laundromat for a few weeks before we decided it was probably easier if we bought a washing machine, a television and a few other basics to get us by.

Nana wanted to have a look around our new place so I drove her up from the Gold Coast for a visit. She provided some valuable living tips for us, three guys who really had little idea how to run a household. Nana had been doing it for decades so she knew how to get us into good habits. I was still reliant on Nana as my only connection outside of football. I spent Christmas 2006 with her, driving down to her townhouse and spending a few days there. Christmas was a quiet affair – just me and Nana around the table – but I really cherished those quiet days. We would head to the beach for a walk, take a trip to the shops and otherwise just spend time together in the house watching TV shows and talking. I was growing closer to her as the years went on and I loved watching Nana become so interested in my footy. She had never been a big sports fan but she converted quickly to rugby league as she watched me play on television most weekends. Nana loved wearing Broncos gear so I made sure I had some merchandise that fitted her. I also brought her a few of my game-worn jerseys to keep. I still wasn't in touch with Mum. She had tried to make contact with me but I wasn't ready for that. It would take time.

Unfortunately for Nana, the 2007 football year wouldn't have the fairytale ending of 2006. We started the year well with a trip to England to play the World Club Challenge, pitting the NRL premiers against the English Super League champions. This was completely new for me; from the heat of a south-east Queensland summer into the cold of an English winter. I had never been on a long-haul flight and I quickly realised what I had been missing as I settled into a business class seat, with plenty of leg room and endless movies to watch. The flight seemed to go quickly, as did the few days in London looking around the usual tourist landmarks before we headed to our base in Manchester. After a warm-up match, we prepared to take on the strong St Helens team, which had cruised through the last Super League season, winning twenty-six of their thirty matches. There were some familiar faces for St Helens – Matt Gidley had played for Newcastle against us in the 2006 finals before moving to England, while Francis Meli and Jason Cayless had been NRL regulars. We led that match until the seventieth minute – I scored a try from a Darren Lockyer kick – but St Helens scored late to win the match.

I distinctly recall the 'rat's tail' that I grew over the course of that off-season. It seemed a good idea at the time – a longer piece of hair growing from the back of my otherwise short haircut that I thought looked very cool – and it didn't stop me from having a reasonable game against St Helens. But Wayne Bennett didn't think much of it. Wayne was ahead of his time when it came to coaching rugby league teams but he had never moved past the 1970s in his preferences for clothing and hairstyles. In his effective way, Wayne told me that my rat's tail had no future. 'Just make sure that thing's gone by Round 1,' he told me at the airport as we headed home from our trip.

The rat's tail was gone by the time we took on the Cowboys in the opening round and it wasn't the only thing missing as we entered a season to largely forget. Johnathan Thurston and

Matt Bowen combined for a winning try in that first game but the result wasn't as concerning as the injuries to Corey Parker and Locky. Corey dislocated his wrist while Locky's ankle problem was the first of his setbacks for 2007 – he would hurt his ankle again midway through the season before a serious knee injury late in the season. We lost to the Warriors in Auckland the following week before a collapse against Penrith – we led by 8 points with two minutes remaining – left us without a win after three matches.

The 2006 premiership felt a long way off after those three rounds. I made a poor start to the season that had all the attributes of second-year syndrome. I had put on five kilograms in the off-season from extra weights sessions because I was sick of being 'rag-dolled' by defenders in my rookie season. The extra weight helped me in collisions but it made me sluggish. I felt as though I had lost pace and that affected my confidence. Wayne could see it and with nowhere to hide in a team that was struggling, he dropped me for the only time in my NRL career. For Round 5, I was sent back to the Aspley Broncos, which had become the Broncos' feeder club in the Queensland Cup. Initially, I was devastated. I had been looking forward to our Round 5 match because the Broncos were playing the Gold Coast Titans for the first time. I considered myself a Gold Coast boy so I wanted to play against the reborn NRL team from the Coast. Instead, I would be playing for Aspley in the curtain-raiser match against the Burleigh Bears. But things don't always work out the way you expect. I went to my first training session for Aspley thinking I would hate it. But it became one of the most memorable training sessions in my early career. Lining up with my new Aspley teammates, I felt like a weight had been lifted off my shoulders. Some of the guys I was training with had full-time jobs and played footy because they loved it. I could feel their energy and I felt the pressure come off me as I trained and played with them. This was why I played footy – because it was a lot of fun to play if you allowed yourself to enjoy it. I played well that weekend and Wayne picked me in the centres for the Broncos' Round 6 game against the Knights.

The Broncos' season never found a rhythm. We were stuck near the bottom of the table in May but three consecutive wins in June pushed us towards the top eight. In the end, our injury toll became too much. For the final matches of the season, we played without Locky, Shaun Berrigan, Brent Tate, Karmichael Hunt and others. We suffered one of our darkest days in the final round of the season when we fell to the Eels 68–22 at Parramatta Stadium. But we qualified for the finals, claiming eighth spot to avoid becoming the first Broncos team since 1991 to miss the post-season. We went to Melbourne for the first week of the finals, collapsing 40–0 to the Storm to end our season. We were so badly affected by injuries that we called in a winger from the Queensland Cup named Alwyn Simpson to start against the Storm. Alwyn travelled to Melbourne without ever training with our team. He had to introduce himself to most of the players in a 24-hour crash course on Broncos football. The season ended badly but we were still good enough to make the finals, which I thought was a huge pass mark for the team. We had battled all year with injuries yet we still finished higher than half of the competition. Others at the club didn't agree with me after so many years of success, but I could see a bright side.

Looking back, it had been a season of learning for me: I had undergone minor ankle surgery in the off-season and recovered from that; I had worked out that bigger wasn't better for me as I experimented with my body weight; I rediscovered my enjoyment for playing footy when I was dropped; I developed a hunger for winning as I rode through some tough losses; and I had gained experience in plenty of positions, playing fullback, wing, centre and on the left and right sides. Every journey has its bumpy rides and 2007 was bumpy for the Broncos – we just had to learn the lessons as a team to ensure it wasn't a wasted season.

Worryingly, 2008 had some early trouble. We began the pre-season with a new-look team after Petero Civoniceva, Brad Thorn, Shaun Berrigan and Dane Carlaw left the Broncos. With Shane Webcke retiring twelve months earlier, we had lost the core of our most recent premiership pack. Peter Wallace, Joel Clinton and Ashton Sims were among our new faces and they began blending in well with our squad as we entered a season when we could operate without the pressure of being the defending premiers. But then a bombshell was dropped that ensured the spotlight would be on us all season. On 4 February, Wayne announced that this would be his last season at the Broncos. He was done after more than two decades at the club. This was huge news. The Broncos were one of the biggest brands in Australian sport and they had only ever had one coach. The media couldn't get enough of the story. They reported the announcement as the final step in a long-running fallout between Wayne and the board. I didn't know the reasons and I didn't ask Wayne why he was going. I was still a quiet, shy twenty-year-old so I wasn't about to bound up to the coach and ask. I knew I would miss him – Wayne had been so important to me in my first two seasons. But I was resigned to the fact that he would go to another club next season and I would continue at the Broncos.

I had signed a two-year deal but the 2009 season was an option in my favour, so I could leave if I wanted a fresh start. As far as I was concerned though, the Broncos were the only club that I wanted to play for. I didn't think about playing anywhere else. My new contract was for $150 000 a season – an increase on the $100 000 I played for in 2007. Wayne pulled me aside in the pre-season to talk about my contract. He explained that only a small percentage of players in the NRL earned $150 000 a season and above – and most of those were representative players. He told me that I needed to understand that my standing at the club was growing as I entered my third season, especially with some of our senior players moving on since our premiership win. The excuses that may have been made for me as a teenager were no longer going to wash as I started the 2008 season with forty-nine games of NRL experience. That conversation stuck with me and it was one of the reasons that I began to change my approach to the game. I began to pay more attention to what I ate. The late-night chicken rolls from the service station and the trips to fast-food restaurants stopped. I developed a better understanding of how foods could help my football, and I combined this with more serious efforts to ensure my body was ready for my third NRL season.

But this new approach didn't apply to all areas of my life. While I was getting serious about watching what foods I ate, I was also becoming a party boy who drank far too much alcohol. I have never been a big drinker, except for a period beginning in 2007 when I began down a dark path that had to be stopped. The Broncos had a drinking culture at that time spread across some of the older and younger players. The 2006 premiership success had sparked some bad habits and this drinking culture was the worst of them. The Broncos were the hottest team in town; free drinks were easy to come by at clubs that wanted us to be seen there and our 2006 grand final win had developed a confidence that fooled us into thinking that we could drink and party and still play good football.

From midway through 2007, we would go out at least twice, sometimes three times, a week. Tuesday nights were always big because we would have Wednesdays off. We would stay out until the doors closed before heading home to sleep in until lunchtime. We would go out after games, riding the adrenaline of the on-field exertion into another 5 a.m. finish. Some players could handle the big nights out – they could drink until dawn was breaking on Wednesday morning and still put in a man-of-the-match performance on Friday night. That wasn't me. I couldn't play my best while I was keeping those hours.

But the lure of being part of this culture was too much for me. I wasn't a leader back then. I was a follower. I hadn't been popular as a kid – I was a bit of an outcast because I was shy and didn't mix easily. All of a sudden, I was playing in the NRL and I was popular. Guys I had looked up to when I was a schoolkid watching footy on television were taking an interest in me. This was my chance to fit in and be part of something. I wanted to be accepted and part of the group so badly that I hung around with guys who I shouldn't have been hanging around with. They were fun guys who weren't breaking any laws but they could live their lives fast and it didn't harm them. I struggled.

Wayne was no fool and he began to notice that things were getting out of hand. He made a decision that players were only allowed to drink on one night each week. This was his balance between letting the players have some responsibility for their decision-making and giving them orders. It was one of Wayne's few decisions on player behaviour that didn't have the desired impact. It made things worse because it meant that we would choose one night each week and make that the biggest night possible. Instead of spreading our drinking across two nights, it was condensed into a one-night event that ended when the pubs shut. We were young, fit, well known in the community, armed with plenty of disposable cash and had access to free alcohol at many places. It was a powderkeg waiting to blow.

Off the field, I made decisions throughout 2007 and into 2008 that were wrong. I'm not proud of some of them and I should have been smarter. I let people down. I put those down as lessons in life. Sometimes you have to learn the hard way. When you're young, you make mistakes regardless of what walk of life you're in. At that stage, I didn't have the parental figure to help me with the transition into responsible adult life. Wayne had given me some great life lessons but he had a family of his own and our relationship wasn't like father and son. I didn't have anyone to answer to at that time and that meant I didn't have to think of consequences. That's not making an excuse for my behaviour. In the end, I made the decisions and I was responsible for them. I was mindful of that period of my life in the latter years of my career as I watched young players come into the league. They still had lessons to learn, but I hoped to pass on anything that could help them avoid some of the mistakes that I made.

The drinking culture within the clubs I played for largely evaporated as social media began to appear in the lives of players. In my early years at the Broncos, you could go out until all hours without having someone with a mobile phone recording and posting footage for the world to see. Soon after that, social media became a platform that forced players to really think about the situations they placed themselves in. Some players were their own worst enemies, posting material on their accounts that became instant headlines. The rise of social media caused a massive adjustment for players thinking about what they did in their spare time.

While this was bubbling along in the background, the Broncos made a promising start to the 2008 NRL season.

For the first time since 2003, the club won its opening three matches. This was a fresh beginning, most obvious when Darren Lockyer played in our opening match against Penrith. It was Locky's first game since recovering from a knee reconstruction and he was the same old Locky. Even with a new halves partner in Peter Wallace, Locky was in charge of the game as we crunched Penrith 48–12. I scored three tries that day and then grabbed one each in our Round 2 defeat of the Roosters in Sydney and our Round 3 win over the Cowboys. That result against the Cowboys was sweet. They had been a handful for us during my time in the NRL but we defeated them 36–2 in front of more than 50 000 fans at Suncorp Stadium on the one hundredth anniversary of the first rugby league game in Queensland. After three matches, the Cowboys had conceded more than 100 points, we were on top of the table and I was the NRL's leading try scorer. I was liking 2008 far more than 2007.

Late in March, news broke that Wayne had signed with St George Illawarra for the next three seasons. I was pleased for Wayne and interested to see who would be taking over at the Broncos for the next season. I didn't spend much time worrying about it because I was planning to be at Brisbane regardless of who was coaching. The Broncos had signed Israel Folau for the next year, which was big news given his performances with Melbourne. I began fielding offers from other teams trying to cash in on the uncertainty created by Wayne's departure. Melbourne Storm made me a decent offer for 2009 to replace Folau. The Storm were the defending premiers and they had an excellent coach in Craig Bellamy and the rising stars of the game in Cameron Smith, Cooper Cronk, Greg Inglis and Billy Slater. It would have been great to play alongside them but I didn't seriously consider it because I had a contract in Brisbane. The Bulldogs also came knocking with a generous offer, but I politely declined.

On the field, our promising start fell away as we lost six of our next eleven games. But there were some bright moments, particularly looking towards the club's future. Denan Kemp and Steve Michaels became regular first graders, which meant a lot to all of us because we were still housemates. With my former Australian Schoolboys teammate Joel Moon also a regular in first grade, I had plenty of familiar faces around me. Unfortunately, Steve's season was over in Round 7 when he suffered a knee injury that required a reconstruction. I was devastated for him because his career was on the way up. He had played in every game for the Broncos in 2007 and earned selection in the Prime Minister's XIII to play Papua New Guinea. Denan made the most of 2008 and scored four tries in a memorable Round 12 game against Parramatta, including a try in the final seconds after swooping on a perfect kick from Locky that broke a deadlock.

Locky was making a surprise return that night from a knee injury, just in time for the opening State of Origin match. Queensland had won the last two series, ending a terrible start to the decade that had included four years without a series win. Locky continued to be Queensland's most important player but his return against Parramatta was a false dawn. Injury would keep him out of the entire series, meaning Queensland would see how good its support cast was under the pressure of Origin. Fortunately, we had the likes of Cameron Smith, Johnathan Thurston, Greg Inglis, Billy Slater, Hodgo, Brent Tate and Israel Folau, who was on debut. Not a bad bunch of names, looking back. But the Blues were revved up by new coach Craig Bellamy and they came out firing in the opening match in Sydney. The Blues won that game 18–10, getting closer to their first series win since 2005.

Origin time was a chance for me to take on more responsibility at the Broncos as our best players headed off on representative duty. That meant I would play fullback or centre as the club saw how the so-called 'Baby Broncos' measured up with the big names away. A week after Origin I, we headed to the XXXX Brewery for our annual signing day. We had hundreds of items to sign for sponsors, so the Broncos helped us make a day of it by encouraging us to wear casual clothes, have a few beers and even enjoy karaoke in between signing sessions. I was a terrible singer. I drove my car that day, parking it near the brewery so I could have a few beers and return the next day to collect it. Unfortunately, I didn't read the fine print on the street sign indicating there was every chance my car would be towed the next day when parking restrictions kicked in.

I returned the next morning to find my car had indeed been towed, so a friend gave me a lift to the towing yard to collect it. On the way there, the Broncos' managing director, Bruno Cullen, rang me.

'Darius, congratulations, you've been selected to play for Queensland in Origin II,' Bruno told me in his deadpan style.

'You must be joking, Bruno. You've got the wrong bloke,' I replied.

Bruno told me he never joked about such things and I was indeed selected for Queensland, one of ten positional or player changes to the Maroons team that played in the opening match. I was stunned. I was playing for Queensland? I had never given it a thought. At the beginning of each year, Queensland picked an Emerging Origin squad to go into camp. I had never been a part of that. I had played well for the Broncos but didn't think I had played well enough for Origin selection. Nana kept in her scrapbook a newspaper article quoting Locky's surprise at my selection. He wasn't as surprised as me. Fortunately, Locky added that he had no doubt that I was up to Origin standard, although I wasn't feeling as confident. I rang Nana to tell her that I had been picked to play on the left wing, which meant that Nana would be adding a Maroons shirt to her wardrobe. She still loved wearing the gear of the teams that I played in.

We went into camp for Origin II, which was to be played at Suncorp Stadium on Wednesday, 11 June. I had to introduce myself to a few people including Mal Meninga, the Queensland legend who was in his third season as Origin coach. Mal congratulated me and asked me if I had been confident of selection. I told him that I was stunned, which seemed to surprise Mal because he said I had been playing well. As a perfectionist, I had no choice but to talk myself down. I was always trying to attain perfection, which of course wasn't possible, so I was my harshest critic, even when I was selected for Queensland.

I was a bit too young to remember Mal playing for the Canberra Raiders, Queensland and Australia, but I would watch enough of his highlights in the following years to understand just how good he was on the field. To be honest, I was bloody terrified of Mal. I was still a young, shy bloke so meeting new people wasn't easy. Especially people like Mal. He was physically imposing, his record was outstanding and he scared the hell out of me when he spoke about how much we should hate New South Wales. Mal wanted us to understand that Origin was only born in 1980 because Queensland had been treated so badly by the Blues for so many years. Before Origin, the annual interstate matches involved players representing the state in which they were playing club football. This created a situation in which a bunch of Queenslanders representing wealthy Sydney clubs would wear blue jerseys and beat up on their home state. Mal played for Queensland in the last year of the old format before he played in the very first Origin match on his twentieth birthday.

Mal brought those stories to a new generation, and to drive the point home he had some help from the infamous 2000 series when the Blues made fun of the Maroons in a record 56–16 win in Sydney. After a late try in that match, the Blues celebrated by launching an imaginary grenade that ended with their players falling to the ground in a mock explosion. That one moment was the perfect incentive for the Maroons old guard that made up that 2008 coaching staff. We had Mal, Allan Langer, Kevin Walters, Trevor Gillmeister, Jason Hetherington and Gavin Allen – all former Maroons players who now had the grenade moment as new evidence to prove to the modern generation what New South Wales really thought of us. They were arrogant, they thought they were better than us, and they always wanted to work the system for their own benefit. Mal would swear and storm about the change rooms as he motivated us, prowling around in front of photos of the players who had been before us. He told us stories of the outrageous behaviour of New South Wales towards Queensland. He told us of the huge sacrifices that had been made by players before us. Above all, Mal convinced us that it was all about the Queensland jersey and playing for Queenslanders. It worked for me. I went into my first Origin camp without any strong feelings against New South Wales, but I left thinking that the Blues were evil.

I didn't have to wait long to taste success against them. I will never forget the roar as I ran on to Suncorp Stadium for my first Origin match. I thought the crowd noise for my first Broncos game in 2006 was the most deafening sound I had heard. It was nothing compared to the noise that greeted us as we ran on to the most famous ground in rugby league. The roar told us everything we needed to know – this was a must-win game and the crowd would be with us for every moment. We fired them up with some bruising tackles on the Blues in the opening minutes and they were singing in the seventh minute with our first try. The movement started deep in our territory as the ball was sent to Greg Inglis playing left centre. G.I. had a perfect body shape in 2008 – he was powerful with lightning speed – and he took the ball, beat his opposite, Mark Gasnier, fended winger Steve Turner like he was a featherweight and then passed to me for an easy try. In the twentieth minute, we were at it again as G.I. made another break, racing forty metres before he again passed to me for a twenty-metre sprint for my second try. I had been in Origin for twenty minutes and I had two tries. This was fun. After I placed the ball for my second try, a Blues defender dived on me, dropping his knees into my backside and corking one of my muscles. Yep, Mal was right. These Blues were evil.

Being a night game, Nana didn't come up to watch my first Origin match. I would have loved her to be there but it was too difficult for her to get back to a hotel for the night, given that she would not be able to make the trip home to the Gold Coast. As it turned out, I didn't need to worry about Nana – she had everything organised at her place. Former Newcastle legend Paul Harragon was then working for Channel Nine's *The Footy Show* and he arranged with Nana to bring a film crew to record her as she watched the game on television. Nana was the perfect interview subject and they filmed plenty of good footage of her cheering as I scored those two early tries. When I watched it later, I enjoyed seeing Nana so happy, but on the night of the game I had no idea that she was being filmed.

I had heard about the intensity of Origin from players who spoke about how the speed of the game left them breathless. They warned that I had to be prepared because this would be a huge step above NRL. To be honest, I didn't notice it in my first game. The first ten minutes had some huge tackles, but we won 30–0 so we were running downhill that night. My experienced teammates said that they felt the match wasn't as intense as previous Origin games that they had played. They told me not to think of this as normal because Origin was the fastest pace of all.

They were right. The decider in Sydney was the most intense match I had played in up until that stage of my career. We took in the same team from Game II, including Scott Prince and Johnathan Thurston in the halves, while the handy three-quarter line was made up of G.I., Brent Tate and Israel Folau. The Blues made changes, including introducing Mitchell Pearce at halfback for his Origin debut at age nineteen. It was a huge call for a teenager. I wasn't much older but I didn't have the spotlight of the halfback duties on me; I knew Mitchell would be playing under pressure. Mal was at his very best for this game. He told us that history was against us – only four teams had won deciders away from home since Origin began almost thirty years ago. We would have around 80 000 people screaming against us at a ground that hadn't been kind to us – we had won only one of our previous thirteen matches at the Olympic Stadium. It was the venue of the famous Blues' grenade celebration, so Mal made sure we remembered that as we prepared to play.

We started well as Israel pounced on a dropped bomb by Anthony Quinn to score in only the fifth minute. But the Blues scored ten minutes later through Matt Cooper to take an 8–4 lead. The twenty-second minute would produce a piece of magic that would live long after the game. J.T. had the ball fifteen metres in front of the Blues' posts when he kicked a crossfield bomb into Israel's right corner. The kick was brilliant and the reception was even better. Israel soared above Anthony Quinn, catching the ball before falling awkwardly, meaning he was upside down when he had to plant the ball for a try. What a moment. Israel was changing football at that time because crossfield kicks were becoming serious weapons and teams across the NRL were trying to work out how high-flying wingers could do the same as him. But the Blues led 10–8 at half-time and their fans were excited.

We levelled the scores with a penalty goal five minutes into the second half before the intensity lifted another level: the Blues had a try disallowed; our forward Michael Crocker was concussed when a clearing kick hit him in the head; and then a serious scuffle broke out. It was going to take a moment of brilliance from either team to break the deadlock and J.T. delivered. In the sixty-sixth minute, he slid across the defensive line until he was between Blues prop Brett White and Mitchell Pearce. J.T. knew that he had Brett beaten for pace so he threw a dummy that sent Mitchell towards G.I., enabling J.T. to scorch across the halfway line before delivering a pass to Billy Slater for a superb try. And that was the difference in the match. We won 16–10, securing Queensland's third successive Origin series win.

That win was an exciting moment but I didn't understand how special it was, coming so early in my career. I enjoyed seeing how my teammates reacted; some had played in losing eras, so a third consecutive series was a big moment for them. My first Origin series gave me a glimpse into the professionalism of Cameron Smith and Billy Slater. I took note of how dedicated they were away from the field. Everything they did seemed to be to the highest possible standard – their diets, their stretching, their warm-ups and warm-downs – and they had an insatiable curiosity for anything that may help them become better footballers. They were about so much more than training drills and game plans – they looked for an edge in any possible element of their games. That stuck with me and I wanted to learn more about this approach.

At that stage of 2008, life was pretty good. But I had learnt that rugby league was a great leveller and I was about to get a bruising reminder. I had just finished a training session at the Broncos when Wayne pulled me aside and asked me about my plans for the next season. I had a contract with the Broncos, so I told Wayne that I would be staying put. He told me that I had better go upstairs to meet with manager Andrew Gee because he had news for me. I wasn't sure what Wayne was getting at, but Andrew told it to me straight: my time at the Broncos was almost done. I was welcome to stay for the next year but I would be finished after that. I was not in the Broncos' plans beyond 2009. I was stunned. In my two and a half years at the Broncos, I had played in a premiership-winning team, I had been in a winning Origin series and I had barely missed a first-grade match. Andrew didn't tell me why the Broncos were cutting me loose and, to this day, I still don't know the real reason why. Maybe there was a combination of factors – I knew Israel Folau was putting pressure on their salary cap and they had a huge opinion of Steve Michaels so perhaps they thought I wasn't needed. I wasn't a great promotional asset for the Broncos because I was so shy that I hated going out to club functions. In 2008, I had to do my first school visit on my own as a Broncos player, but I withdrew at the last minute because I was too nervous. It wasn't ideal but it was hardly a sackable offence.

Andrew told me that while I had a contract for next season, the Broncos were happy for me to move to another club. That sealed the end of my stay at the Broncos. If they didn't want me, I didn't want to remain there. It was devastating because I had always craved acceptance. The Broncos gambled on me in 2006 and had been very loyal to me until that day. I had wanted to repay them and had made no plans to leave. I went downstairs to see Wayne, and spoke to him with tears in my eyes. I had no idea what to do. I was being cut when most teams had long ago locked away their playing lists for 2009. There wouldn't be many positions available. It occurred to me that maybe I should have taken that Storm contract earlier in the year, but Melbourne had moved on and that door was now closed. Wayne calmed me down, and told me that he would be happy for me to join him at the Dragons. There was an opportunity there as Mark Gasnier was leaving the club, opening a spot in the centres.

It didn't take long for the news to get out that my days at the Broncos would soon be over. Speculation then began in the media about where I would end up. St George Illawarra loomed as the favourites because of Wayne. Broncos-related stories always seemed to generate more headlines in Queensland than other topics and my departure was no different. A few journalists even rang Nana to ask her if she knew whether I was going to the Dragons. She would take their call and talk to them because she was a nice lady. She didn't understand how the media worked and that the journalists were only trying to get a story. That really annoyed me. I felt that journalists crossed a boundary by essentially tricking her into helping them with a story. My Dragons negotiations were organised by my new manager, George Mimis, who would become a significant part of my NRL career. The offer from the Dragons was very attractive – it was a far better deal than the Broncos had offered for 2009 but it just happened to be a long way away for someone who had grown up in south-east Queensland.

The Broncos' decision to cut me taught me a very important lesson: rugby league is a business. Pure and simple. Some players get to be one-club servants with the advantages that can hold, but that wouldn't happen to me. In about three months, I would be living in Wollongong and playing for the Dragons. I didn't have a soft spot for the Dragons – I had always cheered for the Broncos – but they would soon be my team. I would be completely on board and desperate to win any game in which I played.

While this was happening, I was trying to focus on the Broncos' drive to the finals. I didn't have a problem focusing on the games ahead because, as always, playing and practising football were my distractions from serious events in my life. We lost our first game after the Origin series but then reeled off three consecutive wins to move into fifth place on the ladder. We were beginning to play well, with shades of our 2006 season. We then lost two games in a row before unleashing three straight wins to close the regular season.

The finals arrived and they were special for Wayne because they would be his last matches as Broncos coach. After twenty-two seasons, Wayne was heading off and the media were obsessed with how he would leave the club – as a winner, with another Wayne-inspired fairytale ending, or after a finals loss? We went to the Sydney Football Stadium in the first week of the finals, taking on the fourth-placed Sydney Roosters. We were back at our favourite finals hotel at Bondi, and we were confident we could beat the Roosters. But again we found ourselves in trouble, this time down 8–16 after an intense first half. It was real finals football and our forwards were hurting at half-time. But we started our comeback with a cracking try in the second half, as the ball passed through thirteen sets of hands before my housemate Denan Kemp scored. David Stagg's try a few minutes later gave us a lead we never relinquished.

We were happy with that win but there was a problem – we had to face the Melbourne Storm in week two. The minor premiers had been stunned by the New Zealand Warriors in the first week of the finals. It was the first time that an eighth-placed team had beaten the top team in the NRL's old finals system. As you could imagine, the Storm didn't take that loss well. It sent them to Brisbane to play us in a semifinal, and they were cranky about losing the home-ground advantage. We weren't fussed about being 'rewarded' for our win with a game against the minor premiers, but the media were loving it. Two teams that had a huge rivalry, Wayne Bennett against his former assistant coach Craig Bellamy, and a likely grand final berth up for grabs because Cronulla awaited the winner in the preliminary final and they were running on empty.

I wasn't emotional about the prospect of my last game with the Broncos. I didn't think like that – I was more excited about the game and the chance to play against the Storm again. The match delivered everything – this was real finals footy, with intensity throughout. We led with two minutes remaining, taking the ball out from our line with victory in sight. We would work through the tackle count, kick for touch and then take our time packing a scrum. That would leave Melbourne with a few seconds to perform a miracle. They got their miracle, it just came earlier than anticipated when a huge tackle by Sika Manu jolted the ball from Ashton Sims' grasp not far out from our line. Within a second, we had gone from winding down to scrambling as the Storm spread the ball. They pushed it to their left side where Greg Inglis scored in the final minute, breaking the hearts of the massive crowd at Suncorp Stadium. A potentially famous win against the Storm had become a devastating night.

What a way to end my time at the Broncos. I felt like that was the end of my time at the club that I had grown up supporting. I wasn't too emotional though – I had put the shutters up and switched my mind to moving to Wollongong in the coming weeks. But I would have a pleasant surprise before then when I was named as a replacement in the Australian squad for the World Cup in October. Justin Hodges and Brett Stewart withdrew from the squad and selectors named me and Karmichael Hunt as replacements. I made my debut against the Papua New Guinea Kumuls on a steamy night in Townsville. My jersey was presented by Laurie Daley, whose speech about his days playing for Australia only got me worried. He left me thinking that the Kumuls would be the hardest men I had ever played and that I would be feeling this match for days. My pride in playing for my country was replaced by concerns that I was about to run into men who made the Easter Island statues feel soft. Laurie was right – the collisions were tough – but we won that game 46–6 to advance to the knockout stages of the World Cup. I didn't play again in that series but I enjoyed the experience and the honour of playing for my country.

That ended one of the most eventful years of my NRL career. I had played State of Origin and for my country. I had been sacked by my club. I had fallen into a drinking culture that led me to make bad decisions. I had to learn the lessons from that year. Looking back, I didn't learn enough. There would be more to come. I packed my things and headed for Wollongong, leaving my comfort zone for good.

CHAPTER 6

The cracks appear

THE BEST THING ABOUT MOVING TO ST GEORGE ILLAWARRA in 2009 was that I wouldn't be facing any more losses to the Dragons. Since I had made my NRL debut, I had played six games against the Dragons and lost them all. We weren't even close in some of those games, even when the Broncos had been in great form. The Broncos had finished ahead of the Dragons on the ladder in each of the last three seasons – in 2007, the Dragons won only nine games and two were against Brisbane. Sometimes, you just have a bogey team that you find impossible to beat. The Dragons were the Broncos' bogey team. I could analyse statistics to find a reason but I'd be wasting my time. Sometimes there are no reasons. That's just how sport goes.

Over the decades, the Dragons had been the bogey team for plenty of rivals. I didn't know much about the Dragons except for the obvious: they were the most famous club in Australian rugby league history; they had some of the most passionate fans; and they once won eleven consecutive premierships. That still sounds incredible. In one of those years they won premierships in all three senior grades. I wondered how much of the Dragons' tribal following stemmed from the memories of that dynasty, for better or for worse. That golden run had to sustain the club because in 2009, the Dragons hadn't won a premiership for thirty years. My new teammates Brett Morris and Dean Young were the living reminder of the Dragons' premiership drought. Their fathers had played in the club's last premiership team – Craig Young was the captain and Steve Morris was the flying winger. It had been a while.

The Dragons represented the St George and Illawarra regions following the merger of two traditional clubs in 1999. That meant that Wayne Bennett, as the new coach, could base us in St George or the Illawarra. Fortunately, he chose to base us in the Illawarra's largest city of Wollongong – a coastal location without the bustle of Sydney. Wayne could go about his new coaching stint away from the pressures of Sydney, and he quickly became a common sight on the streets of Wollongong as he went for his many runs. My Broncos teammate Nick Emmett had also moved to the Dragons and set himself up in Wollongong in a unit. Nick asked me to move in with him, which suited me fine. I quickly enjoyed Wollongong and felt settled there in my first move out of Queensland.

The only downside was the challenge of getting home to visit Nana and my friends. During the season, I would make the most of each Friday night game, jumping on a plane in Sydney first thing on Saturday morning for a flight to Brisbane. I would stay with mates through Saturday and head down to the Gold Coast on Sunday morning to see Nana. I'd catch a flight out of Gold Coast Airport on Sunday night and be ready for training on Monday. Those weekends went by in a flash but the trips home helped to settle my homesickness.

One of the pleasant surprises in signing with St George Illawarra was playing with Wendell Sailor. He was the first Broncos player that I really looked up to as a young bloke, dressed in my pyjamas and watching games on television. Wendell was in the twilight of his career at the Dragons, turning thirty-five during the 2009 season. But he was still fast – the old bloke was the second fastest in our forty-metre sprints in the pre-season. They say you should never meet your idols but Wendell couldn't have been better to me. And he was a great influence on the team because he was one of the last real characters of the game. He could make light of any situation, dancing in a tense dressing room before kick-off or stirring up opposition players to put them off their game. During a game against his great Newcastle rival Adam MacDougall in 2009, big Dell scored two tries. After each try, Dell would hold a finger up to let MacDougall know how many tries he had scored. The crowd loved it, the players felt calm and Wayne privately thought it was hilarious. Wayne seemed to really enjoy the players who acted in ways totally opposite to his reserved public persona.

When I agreed to move to the Dragons, I didn't give much thought to their premiership chances in 2009. That hadn't influenced my decision because I really didn't have a choice of clubs after the Broncos left it relatively late in the previous season to tell me I could look elsewhere. I wasn't sitting back comparing offers from teams of differing standards. But the Dragons were well placed to make a run into September. They had made the finals in 2008 before recruiting well for the new season. The club had lost its legendary centre Mark Gasnier and frontline players Josh Morris and Jason Ryles but there were talented signings in the likes of Jeremy Smith, Nathan Fien, Michael Weyman and veteran Luke Priddis.

We got the first test of our standing in Round 1, travelling to Melbourne to take on a Storm team that had been smashed 40–0 by Manly in the 2008 grand final. The Storm were up for this match but so was our new-look team, taking Melbourne into extra time in a positive start to the season. The game ended in a similar way to my previous NRL game – Greg Inglis had the final say. This time, he kicked a field goal a few minutes into extra time to end the match. The performance was enough to suggest the Dragons could be competitive in 2009.

For the first time in my career – and Wayne's career for that matter – we took on the Broncos in Round 4 in Brisbane. The game received plenty of media coverage because of Wayne's return to the club that he had coached for twenty-one years. If Wayne was worked up, we didn't know as players. As always, Wayne could hide any personal thoughts from us. I knew we were in for a tough night when Wendell was booed every time he touched the ball. That unsettled me because Brisbane fans didn't have a reputation for booing former players. I was lucky – they didn't seem to care too much when I touched the ball. Although maybe that was a bad reflection on me.

For the first time in a Broncos versus Dragons match, I was on the winning team as we completed a solid 25–12 victory. The night was uneventful for me. I wasn't too emotional at playing my former team and I didn't go out there with a point to prove. I just aimed to play well and to continue building our combinations. When the Dragons defeated Parramatta the following week, we had a 4–1 win–loss record and sat on top of the table. I was enjoying my time with the club and was settled at fullback, rapt to finally have the No. 1 jersey.

I would return to the wing for the representative season, starting with the Test against New Zealand at Suncorp Stadium. My form with the Dragons had helped me to win selection in the top Australian team for the first time. And the match was special because the Kangaroos backline was made up entirely of Queenslanders. That had not happened since 1924. I was in the No. 5 jersey and my backline partners were: 1 Billy Slater; 2 Israel Folau; 3 Greg Inglis; 4 Justin Hodges; 6 Darren Lockyer; and 7 Johnathan Thurston. Our backline contributed all of our thirty-eight points that night in our comfortable win. Hodgo and J.T. scored two tries each, Israel, Billy and I scored a try while J.T. kicked five goals.

That performance gave us plenty of confidence that Queensland could win another Origin series, which was starting a few weeks later. Given that I had played for Australia, I probably shouldn't have been worried about being selected for Queensland. But Wendell was playing very well for the Dragons and, if they picked me from nowhere last year, what would stop them doing the same for another player in 2009? Such is the life of a perfectionist – the downside always looms larger than the upside. I was also worried because after having tasted Origin in 2008 – however surprising I felt my selection was – I now knew what I would be missing if I wasn't picked. So I was relieved to get a phone call to say I had been selected for a series that would begin in Melbourne for the first time in Origin history, followed by a game in Sydney. We would have to wait until Game III to get to Brisbane.

That Origin series belonged, in many ways, to Greg Inglis. He was superb in the opening match, showcasing all of his skills as we scored three tries in the first seventeen minutes and then pushed on for a 28–18 win over an inexperienced Blues team. G.I. was a freak and it was a privilege to play outside him. He created so many opportunities with his speed, strength and power and he was at the peak of those skills in 2009, with a body shape that was perfectly balanced for maximum efficiency across those areas.

He was the best all-round athlete that I played with or against. He had the physical attributes but he was also a smart player. He would make split-second decisions in a game that created moments of brilliance. He played mostly at centre but he also played for Queensland and Australia at fullback. He won a Clive Churchill Medal at five-eighth for Melbourne in 2007. He was simply brilliant at his best.

I got to know G.I. very well as we became Origin roommates. Our room wasn't the party room. G.I. was relaxed, easygoing and a quiet roommate. He loved a chat, loved a laugh and nothing seemed to faze him. G.I. never liked being the centre of attention but he enjoyed hanging out with others. I've always known him as a very proud Indigenous man and someone who is passionate about Aboriginal and Torres Strait Islander issues and outcomes. His friendship was one of the stronger friendships of my playing career.

I always thought that I was blessed to play for Queensland when I did. I was at the end of a left edge that featured G.I. and J.T. playing inside me. The Blues would sometimes need to commit two defenders to stop J.T. as he jinked and stepped. That often meant G.I. was able to break free, so defenders would have to rush across to stop him if J.T. found him. And that would leave me with plenty of room on the left wing, loving the fact that these two magicians inside me were causing so much trouble.

That's how Game I ended as G.I. stepped off his right foot, dummied and then threw an overhead basketball pass for me to score, sealing the result. He posted the first try of Game II in Sydney, bulldozing over the line as we scored three times in the opening twenty-five minutes. But we would have to wait until Cameron Smith picked up a loose ball to score in the seventy-ninth minute to ensure that we were the first team to win four consecutive Origin series. And we had to do it without G.I. for all but twenty-two minutes of that match after his jaw was fractured from a swinging Blues arm in a tackle. He recovered in time for Game III although we couldn't hold off New South Wales that night, missing out on a clean sweep.

The final two minutes of that match ensured that this Queensland team would never be complacent, despite four consecutive series wins. The game was out of our reach when our veteran prop Steve Price and Storm prop Brett White began swapping punches. Pricey was concussed by a punch and was falling to the ground when he was tackled by Blues forward Trent Waterhouse. While Pricey lay motionless on the ground, my Dragons teammate Justin Poore lifted him and dropped him back to the ground again. All hell broke loose. Waterhouse was sent off. We received a penalty, which led to us taking a tap and kicking the ball back to the Blues. Another scuffle began, resulting in Sam Thaiday and my Dragons teammate Ben Creagh being sin-binned.

The series was over a few seconds later and Queensland emerged as the champions again, but the actions of the final moments made us feel that we had been wronged. Forget about celebrating as we lifted the Origin shield after the match – we wanted revenge in 2010. It was perfect for our coach Mal Meninga, who wouldn't have to worry about complacency the following year. Mal told us over and over again how much the Blues hated us, and the Blues kept finding ways to prove Mal right. That was a central part of our successful Origin run.

The move to the Dragons had worked out very well for me in 2009 as we sat on top of the table heading into the final rounds of the season. But my maturing as a football player wasn't being matched by greater maturity as a person. I was struggling with my moods but that had been hidden by my performances on the field. The Origin camps were becoming my favourite times of the year, when I could disappear from the reality of the world. It was an environment in which I didn't have to worry about too much, including my deteriorating mental health.

I gave the first public insight into my mental health with one of the most infamous interviews in the modern NRL era. On Tuesday, 18 August, a few days after I felt I had played poorly in a loss to Canberra, I was asked by the Dragons media manager to do an interview with journalists after training. This should not have been a big deal – each club usually offered one player or a member of the coaching staff to speak with journalists. And we were playing the Broncos a few days later so journalists wanted to ask me about taking on my former team and some of my Origin teammates. I told the media manager that I wouldn't do it, but she reminded me of the Dragons' obligations under NRL rules to offer a press conference. It was my turn and I had to do it. So over I went, and here's what happened:

Question: 'Up against the Broncos, excited about facing your old mates?'
Answer: 'Yeah, can't wait.'
Question: 'That excited?'
Answer: 'Yep.'
Question: 'Did you watch them play last week?'
Answer: 'No, I didn't.'
Question: 'What's the strategy going into the game?'
Answer: 'We'll decide that on Wednesday I suppose.'

Question: 'Happy to score another try, it was a good one?'

Answer: 'Yeah, it was good, ay.'

Question: 'Second one of the season, it's taken a little while, you must be keen to be coming into form at the right time of the season.'

Answer: 'No it was good.'

Question: 'What are your thoughts on the way your team is going at the moment Darius?'

Answer: 'Um, yeah, it was pretty good, ay.'

Question: 'Are you fair dinkum?'

Answer: 'Yeah.'

Journalist: 'Waste of time.'

That was it. All forty-three seconds of a trainwreck that would impact me for years to come. The only things worse than my answers were my facial expression and tone of voice. I clearly didn't want to be there. My profile had risen within rugby league in recent years but people still didn't know much about me. They now had something on which to form an opinion about me – a terrible interview that made me look smug and silly.

There were two key reasons, rather than excuses, for my behaviour that day. We had lost to Canberra the previous weekend and I had let in a late try. I was feeling as though I had let the team down. Wayne had pulled me aside and told me that my mistake didn't cost us the game, especially considering I had scored a seventy-metre try, but I didn't have the ability to process that. I focused on the negatives and I focused on them for days.

I was also still finding it hard to trust people. If I didn't know and trust someone – and the people who ticked those boxes for me were few in number – I wouldn't give them the time of day. One of my biggest trust issues revolved around the media. I simply didn't like them and certainly didn't trust them. The fact that they would call Nana for information had really annoyed me. I struggled to get over that. Given this, I was always going to find it hard to trust people who barely knew me yet were continually making comments about me.

The main reason for my press conference behaviour, though, was my growing struggle to deal with my life off the field. The issues that I had continued to suppress, hidden by my dedication to football, were starting to bubble up, and perceptive observers may have noted that for the first time. Wayne sat me down and told me that club officials were very unhappy with the interview. But Wayne admitted he couldn't criticise me given that he was known for his short press conferences. My teammates thought it was hilarious. Players from around the NRL were texting me to say how funny it was. We were having a Dragons team dinner the next night when my interview was played on television near where we were sitting. Everyone laughed and congratulated me. The only real consequence for my actions was that I had to wear a 'Goose of the week' T-shirt to training a few days later – and my teammates thought that was funny, too.

Looking back on it, I feel very embarrassed about that interview. I was a young guy without the tools to deal with my declining mental health and that interview was a step down a worrying path. One of the problems that I had was that I still had no one to answer to in my life. There were no consequences. I could do whatever I felt like within the bounds of the law. If I wanted to be a smart-arse, who was going to stop me? My teammates would laugh about it, my coach wasn't the type to read a riot act to me, Nana would always support me and I hadn't spoken to Mum for years. Plus, I was playing good football so it wasn't like my career was at risk from one smart-mouthed interview. I didn't have a checkpoint and I had no idea how badly I needed one.

The loss to Canberra was the first of three consecutive losses as we began stumbling towards the finals. This was another post-Origin slump that rivalled our 2006 struggles at the Broncos. We hit our lowest point in Round 25 when we were hammered 41–6 by South Sydney, a team that was out of finals contention. That was a huge blow for Dragons fans who had so enjoyed 2009. We had gone from certainties for the minor premiership a few weeks earlier to struggling to make the top two. And our final match was against Parramatta, who were on a seven-game winning streak. But we played at home at Kogarah Oval and smashed the Eels 37–0. There you have it – beaten by 35 points the week before by a team that wouldn't make the finals and then putting 37 unanswered points on the hottest team in the league the next week.

Just like that, our confidence was back. We were the minor premiers, claiming the J.J. Giltinan Shield, and our Dragons fans were again getting excited about our premiership chances. The first week of the finals looked promising to those fans –

we were up against the Eels again. Same opposition. Same ground. How could the fans not be confident? But the NRL is a league for the hungry teams. If you're 5 per cent off your normal level of intensity and your opposition is playing well, you'll probably lose. The competition can be that close. And when we took on Parramatta again, they were far hungrier than us. We were bloated after a week of feeling good about ourselves, and the Eels were desperate. They also had Jarryd Hayne – a player who could be as devastating as G.I. when he was in the zone. He was that day. We lost 25–12, placing us into a sudden-death showdown with the Broncos at Suncorp Stadium the following week.

We were never in that match against the Broncos, a game that saw my old Broncos House mate Dave Taylor play one of his better NRL matches. I'm sure the Dragons fans were devastated by the loss. We had shown so much promise that year but lost five of our last six games to bounce out of the finals in straight sets. After the game, Wayne said something prophetic. He told us that we hadn't suffered a late-season fade-out. Instead, we had learnt a very important lesson on the way to winning a premiership. Wayne was right.

CHAPTER 7

A year to remember

ON THE SURFACE, IT WOULD SEEM THAT KAYLA HEATHCOTE and I had very, very little in common. Kayla was a New Zealander, the oldest child of a Samoan mother and Scottish father who were seventeen and twenty years old when she was born. She grew up in Wellington and moved to the Gold Coast in 2009. Kayla appeared to be a confident woman who could hold a conversation with almost anyone. She was smart, witty and inquisitive. She had no interest in football. Absolutely none. And she didn't care much for strange men who walked up to her in nightclubs.

But that's what I did in April 2010, a few hours after the Dragons had played the Titans on the Gold Coast. Clearly, I had been drinking because I found the courage to walk up to a stunning woman and told her I'd like to buy her a drink. Kayla wasn't so pleased.

'I can buy my own drink. Why do I need you to buy me a drink?' she responded.

And so my relationship with Kayla Heathcote began. I guess it could only improve from there. Kayla did let me plead my case to buy her a drink and we began to talk, although I'm not sure I had much to give Kayla that night apart from my smile and my undivided attention. I learnt that Kayla had a real estate job and she lived on her own. She had been on the Gold Coast for six months and her mother and stepfather lived not far from her. It sounded as though she had her life under much better control than I did. Kayla knew nothing about the NRL and didn't seem interested in learning much about it. But we found we had one thing in common – we were both born in 1987. That was good enough for me.

We went our separate ways from the nightclub that night and when Kayla returned home, she searched my name on the internet. She didn't remember my last name or what code of football I played – Kayla's friend told her that she thought I played for the Sydney Swans AFL team. So, she typed 'Darius Sydney Swans' into the search engine and eventually found me, due to my uncommon first name. One of the first results to come up was my infamous interview the previous August, all forty-three seconds of my bumbling, mumbling responses and accompanying comments from online browsers. Not a great start for my chances of building a relationship with Kayla.

I returned to Wollongong the next day and decided to call her. Fortunately, Kayla was happy to speak to me – perhaps the person in the TV interview was so different from the one she met in the nightclub that she wanted to find out why. She was the most beautiful woman I had ever seen and she had an approach to life that I found compelling. Kayla knew how to get straight to the point and she didn't mind asking hard questions. She got things done and she didn't procrastinate. She didn't seek confrontations, however, if one was needed in life, Kayla was fine with that. All of those attributes were the opposite to me. And they were among the reasons I found Kayla so interesting.

She didn't need to be too perceptive to understand that my family life was far from normal. When Kayla asked me about my family, I could only tell her that I had my grandmother Delphine and really no one else. I told her that I didn't know my father, my mother was estranged and my beloved grandfather and uncle had died when I was young. There were no aunties, no living uncles, no cousins and no siblings. But Kayla never flinched at that, which revealed more of her qualities to me. I learnt that Kayla may have been forthright and driven, but she was built on compassion and a belief that everyone was equal. Kayla's football knowledge didn't amount to much more than an awareness of the bad behaviour of some players off the field. She really couldn't have cared less that I had a public profile – in fact, that made her worried about starting a relationship with me. That reluctance was the reason that, after our first meeting, Kayla and I didn't see each other for about three months. We spoke on the phone a lot but, every time I went back to the Gold Coast to see Nana, there seemed to be a reason that Kayla couldn't meet up with me.

Eventually, Kayla's mum, Pepa, helped me out without me knowing. Pepa told Kayla that, if I was still showing interest after this length of time, perhaps she should meet up with me for a coffee. So, in the winter, we met each other for the first time since that brief encounter at the nightclub in April. We hit it off and, not long after, Kayla visited me for a weekend in Wollongong. She wasn't interested in watching my games on television, because rugby league didn't interest a girl from New Zealand, but she was happy to see if we could develop a relationship. That suited me fine.

Those months in 2010 were a happy part of my life. I was falling in love with Kayla and my football was better than ever. The Dragons' win over the Titans on the Gold Coast on the night I met Kayla was followed by huge wins over the Roosters and Cronulla. We won seven of our first eight matches to sit on top of the table. In those eight games we had given up an average of 8.8 points a match, while scoring 25. But we were still criticised for our attack, which had commentators speculating whether we had enough all-round skills to end the Dragons' 31-year premiership drought.

The 2010 premiership had been blown wide open in late April when the Melbourne Storm salary-cap scandal was uncovered. The Storm had apparently been using two sets of books to record their player payments – one set of books containing false figures was provided to the NRL while a second, containing the real figures, was kept in secret by the

Storm. That dossier was uncovered by the NRL and their action was swift and devastating for the Storm. The club's 2007 and 2009 premierships were stripped. They lost their 2006, 2007 and 2008 minor premierships and the 2010 World Club Challenge victory. And, in 2010, they would be playing for no points. The Storm would finish last regardless of how many matches they won that year.

The news rocked the NRL. The Storm were the benchmark of the competition, the team that was consistently the hardest to beat. I thought about the Storm's approach to me in 2008, although it never progressed to the stage of being offered a contract. I knew many of the Melbourne players, especially the likes of Cameron Smith, Greg Inglis and Billy Slater, from our times together in Origin camp. And I knew them to be upstanding people who wouldn't have known about a salary-cap rort.

The news brought out different emotions among NRL players. I felt for the older Parramatta players who had lost the 2009 grand final to the Storm. Some would never get the chance to play in a grand final again and I could understand why they would be upset. The scandal didn't bother me too much. I had played in a winning grand final against the Storm in 2006 and a heartbreaking semifinal loss in 2008. But we'd had a very good chance of winning that match and weren't good enough on the night. Despite this, I wasn't unhappy that the Storm were out of the running in 2010. They would finish with a record of fourteen wins and ten losses, which would only have been good enough for fifth on the ladder.

Every year, Wayne Bennett would break our season down into blocks to help us maintain our focus. Our blocks were going well in 2010 as we claimed the competition lead in Round 5 and never gave it up. The State of Origin period covered a block of six matches in 2010 and it shaped as a challenge, with seven Dragons playing for their states. Neville Costigan joined me in the Queensland team, while five of our teammates – Brett Morris, Matt Cooper, Beau Scott, Michael Weyman and Ben Creagh – were chosen for the Blues. This was Queensland's chance to win a fifth-straight series and the risk of complacency was reduced for three reasons: the Blues would host two games; the Storm players were hungry for their only meaningful wins that year; and the constant questions from journalists about the fiery end to last year's series kept that memory fresh. Then we had another moment that roused our camp into action – Blues assistant coach Andrew Johns was accused of using racist language to his squad when he described Greg Inglis and Israel Folau. Blues winger Timana Tahu left the squad in protest and the news was not taken well by our players. It was another instalment in the Blues' unfailing efforts to provide the Maroons with motivation.

G.I. and Israel scored four tries between them as we won the opening two matches to claim a fifth consecutive series. The first match at the Olympic Stadium was sealed when Johnathan Thurston stripped the ball from Blues captain Kurt Gidley close to the line, handing off a pass to Sam Thaiday for an easy try. We sealed the series in Brisbane with a 34–6 win – the Blues scored their only points in the final minute of that match – before we went back to Sydney to score twice in the last five minutes for a 23–18 victory in Game III. That was our first clean sweep since 1995 and it pleased Mal Meninga who had drilled into us the need to remain focused for the final match. I scored a try in each match that year, making the most of the work of J.T. and G.I. inside me as our backline remained unchanged throughout the series.

At the Dragons, the Origin period began badly when prop Dan Hunt snapped his Achilles tendon in the warm-up for our clash against Canberra. If there was ever a bad sign for this 'block' of matches during Origin time, this was it. Wayne said he had never had a player suffer such a serious injury before a game, adding a fifth injured player to a list of absentees including the Origin players. We lost that game but then surged through the Origin period, with four consecutive wins and an aggregate total of 108–34. We then received news that we hadn't expected – we would be getting a recruit for the second half of the season. Mark Gasnier, one of the best-known Dragons of the modern era, was returning from a rugby union stint in Paris to play with us again. He joined us before the last game of the Origin period – a top-of-the-table home clash with Penrith. Gaz had only three days training with the Dragons and he was rusty, but we knew that he would be a key part of our premiership campaign.

Gaz took back his position at right centre and his presence was critical as we started to build the combinations for a run deep into September. Losses to the Titans and Broncos in consecutive weekends were our only real concern before we won four of our last five matches to claim the minor premiership by two wins. We hosted the Rabbitohs in our final match of the regular season, enabling Wayne to rest five players who had been battling minor injuries before the finals. We cruised past the Rabbitohs 38–24 to end our regular season with seventeen wins and seven losses.

The mood among Dragons fans varied between excitement, tension and dread. They knew that it had been thirty-one years since the club had won a premiership, almost back to those golden years when the Dragons were the most dominant team in any sport anywhere in the world. We had been the best team in the league that season but our fans were still hurting from our collapse in the finals the previous year after claiming the minor premiership. And the media continued to criticise our attack, with some commentators claiming we couldn't win the grand final with our 'boring' style of play. I had always heard that defence wins premierships and our defence had been incredible all season. We had conceded only 299 points during the home-and-away matches for an average of only 12.45 per game. The next-best defensive record belonged to the New Zealand Warriors, with 486 points conceded. But our attacking record of 518 points was only the eighth best that season, which had commentators doubting us. They believed attack was more fashionable than defence in 2010 and questioned how we could continue to weather the offensive onslaughts from our finals opponents.

We didn't have to worry about that in the first week as we kept Manly scoreless in a 28–0 qualifying final win. The match was closer than the scoreline suggests because Manly kept pressuring our line, playing with the freedom of a team that only made the finals because Melbourne was barred from earning points. We put our foot down in the last twenty minutes, pulling away for a win that boosted the confidence of the Dragons fans still bruised from the corresponding match of the last season when we fell to the Eels. That win gave us a week off – a huge advantage as we tried to ensure our players were rested for the preliminary final against the winner of the match between the Raiders and the Wests Tigers in Canberra.

The week off football meant a complete change in pace at the most important time of the season. The familiar pattern of training and playing was put on hold as we had the luxury of taking our time to prepare for our next game. That gave me more time to talk with Kayla, whom I had been seeing more often as the season went on. Our frequent phone calls were mixed with rare meetings in person as I returned home to catch up with Nana. I treasured the time I spent with Kayla and found quickly that I could trust her. She was warm and she was genuine – two traits that definitely helped me when I tried to trust someone. Kayla took my mind off football completely, which was important for me, particularly as we came to the biggest games of the year. There was no thought of Kayla returning to Wollongong to visit as we made our way through the finals. Kayla was busy with her work and life on the Gold Coast, and it would have been a difficult juggle for us to spend time together between training sessions. So, it was back to talking on the phone and texting while we prepared for the preliminary final against the Tigers, who toppled the Raiders by two points in Canberra.

Criticism of the Dragons' attack had not worried me during the season. I knew that our defence was excellent, and we often talked about the fact that if we gave up 12 points or fewer in a game, we would win. I was more concerned about our ability to overcome half-time deficits because that had been a problem for us during the season. The commentators hadn't picked up on this habit of ours, but it was the thing that worried me most as we headed into our preliminary final against the Tigers at the Olympic Stadium. I knew that we had to get off to a good start or we faced a tough night.

The Dragons fans were out in force as more than 71 000 people filled the stadium. That figure was more than the size of the combined crowds for the two preliminary finals in Sydney two years earlier. That showed just how hungry the Dragons supporters were to end this 31-year drought, and they gave us a huge roar as we ran out to take on the Tigers. But we were soon behind after Lote Tuqiri, back in the NRL after his rugby union stint, scored in the left corner in the seventeenth minute to put the Tigers ahead 6–0. We levelled the scores with a try to Jeremy Smith in the twenty-seventh minute, but a try to the Tigers five minutes before half-time meant that we would have to come from behind.

At half-time, I was worried about how we would respond, realising that our two years of team-building in Wollongong, which included winning two minor premierships, hinged on the next forty minutes. We always set our marker to concede no more than 12 points a game, meaning that we had no room for error against a Tigers team that could score long-range tries through the magic of playmaker Benji Marshall. But half-time in matches as tense and important as those belonged to Wayne Bennett. That was when Wayne was at his calmest and that mood flowed through the change rooms as we prepared for the second half. Wayne spoke to us about the Tigers' rushing up in defence to prevent us from finding our danger men. We hadn't adjusted well to the Tigers' plan and Wayne worked with us on ways to cope.

Within ten minutes, we were level at 12-all and feeling confident that we could edge ahead. But the Tigers were relentless that night and we couldn't get into a groove with our attack. It came down to the seventy-fourth minute with a move that we had practised at training a number of times during the previous fortnight. Hooker Nathan Fien knew it was time for a field goal, so ensured our big men were set to provide some distraction for defenders as Jamie Soward took a pass from Nathan for our one shot at victory. Jamie stood about thirty-five metres out and steered through the sweetest field goal in the Dragons' modern history. That gave us the lead for the first time that night, although the Tigers weren't done. With forty seconds to go, they started a movement from their twenty-metre line as Keith Galloway charged down our left side, finding support before a kick bounced towards the tryline. I desperately ran back and collared the ball only a metre or so from the Tigers before tossing it over the dead-ball line. We had overcome that half-time deficit, keeping the Tigers scoreless in the second half for a 13–12 win that booked us a grand final spot against the Sydney Roosters. We were emotional at the end of that game, probably in relief that we hadn't blown another minor premiership and that we had managed to come from behind in a gripping second half.

As always, grand final week was Wayne's favourite time of the year, when he could reach deep into his kitbag to produce something that would motivate his players to perform beyond their best. He created a stir by booking our finals hotel of choice – the Swiss-Grand Resort in the heart of Roosters' territory at Bondi Beach. The media loved the fact we were holed up there, although it wasn't a big deal for us given that we had stayed there the previous weekend. There were many obvious motivations for our team. The massive crowd that attended the preliminary final at the Olympic Stadium had shown us what the grand final meant to them, and while Wayne and I had been at the Dragons for only two years, many in our team had friendships that went back years – they played for each other, as our defensive record showed that year. We also had the motivation to win – Dean Young and Brett Morris, sons of premiership players from 1979, were selected for the grand final.

I approached this grand final differently from 2006, when everything was new in my first season with the Broncos. The three seasons that had passed without a grand final appearance had made me appreciate how hard it was to reach the decider.

It was raining on the day of the game. I looked out the window of the hotel in Roosters country to watch the rain hitting Bondi Beach. That may not have worried our Dragons forwards but, as a fullback who was expected to field all types of kicks while a massive crowd and television audience watched on, the thought of a slippery ball wasn't filling me with confidence.

I spoke to Nana on the phone before the game and she gave me her usual message – good luck and don't get hurt. Kayla had been a great support to me throughout the finals, although she remained on the Gold Coast, watching the match on television.

We were favourites for the match, although the Roosters were the fashionable team for many commentators who admired their dismantling of the Gold Coast Titans in the preliminary final. The Roosters had the likes of Dally M Player of the Year Todd Carney and Mitchell Pearce in the halves, while fullback Anthony Minichiello and captain Braith Anasta added plenty of experience.

The rain stopped when we ran out to play. We needed only seven minutes to score the first try when Jamie Soward's kick found a flying Mark Gasnier centimetres from the dead-ball line. But that was the end of our points in the first half as the Roosters scored twice to take an 8–6 lead into the break. For the second week in a row, we would have to recover from a half-time deficit. The win over the Tigers had given us confidence but this was the grand final – there were the pressures of playing in the most important game of the year and not letting down the tens of thousands of Dragons fans in attendance. The half-time break was unusually quiet in our change room, but it was a quiet caused by our sharp focus rather than us being downcast.

We had to wait only five minutes in the second half to take the lead as we moved the ball to our right edge where Gaz was the main focus of defenders. That enabled me to move into the line and watch defenders run to Gaz as I took the ball and passed to Jason Nightingale for a try in the corner. Jason scored again thirteen minutes later, and this was soon followed by a moment that was extra special for Dragons fans. Dean Young ran off a pass from Nathan Fien at short range to score next to the posts, handing us a 24–8 lead with only sixteen minutes to play. Dean's father, Craig, had led the Dragons to the 1979 premiership so the try, which basically sealed the match, was fitting for our many fans who had waited decades for this night. Nathan's try from dummy half in the seventieth minute provided the final scoreline of 32–8 as we claimed the premiership. In each of our finals in 2010, we had kept our opposition scoreless in the second half. That underlined just how strong our defence was that year.

What a night. I was rapt for the Dragons fans who cherished our win. I had always admired their passion – they also let me know when I didn't play well, but that's fine – and I felt that this result was a reward for them for staying loyal to the club for so long. Over the years, I would learn just how much Dragons fans loved that night. There would be countless times when I would be going about my business, either shopping or having a coffee or the like, and a Dragons fan would come up to me and tell me how much that 2010 premiership meant to them. Helping to bring some joy to fans like that is one of the privileges of playing sport.

My greatest surprise from that night came during the presentation when I was awarded the Clive Churchill Medal as player of the match. Clive's widow, Joyce, presented me with the medal that I had not expected. I showed just how surprised I was by starting my acceptance speech with a long shout of: 'Woooooooo.' Clearly, my football was better than my performance on stage that night. The Churchill Medal meant more to me as each year passed – at the time it was a pleasant surprise but I was more excited about winning the grand final. Other guys in our team deserved to win the medal that night. I've always thought that I received it because I'd had a good season, finishing third in the Dally M voting, and so I was probably in the judges' minds.

The celebrations were long for Dragons fans but short for players as we prepared for the 2010 Four Nations series to close the footy year. I was selected in coach Tim Sheens' squad but I knew that my chances of playing were thin. Tim had told me that I wouldn't play fullback – Billy Slater had that position – and he wanted a specialist to play on the wing, which ruled me out. He was true to his word when Jarryd Hayne pulled out of the squad and Lote Tuqiri was brought in as a replacement to start on the wing with my Dragons teammate Brett Morris.

My fifth season in the NRL had been my best yet. The journey out of my comfort zone two years earlier had resulted in a premiership with the Dragons that I would savour for many years. We had built that premiership on defence and our belief as a team. I was in great physical shape and my body was holding up well despite the number of games that we played that season. It was a year to remember but that wasn't just because of the football. Kayla and I continued our relationship even though we were living in different cities for six months. The best thing that happened to me in 2010 wasn't a premiership or the Clive Churchill Medal. It was meeting Kayla Heathcote one April night on the Gold Coast.

RESILIENCE
2011–2014

CHAPTER 8

Life with Macca

ALEX MCKINNON HAD AN OLD HEAD ON YOUNG SHOULDERS. He was eighteen years old when we first lived together in Wollongong in 2010, but he wasn't a teenager who wanted to stay up late and party. Alex didn't drink or smoke, and he had that touch of country calmness from his upbringing in Aberdeen, a town less than two hours' drive from Newcastle. He had moved to Wollongong when he signed a contract with the Dragons and we ended up sharing a unit together. Alex was almost five years younger than me so I tried to set an example, but he didn't need much advice. Alex could talk to anyone and he always seemed interested in what people had to say. He enjoyed life, enjoyed learning and loved playing and watching football.

There were a few tips I could give Alex: I knew how to cook; I knew how to buy groceries; and I knew how to pay bills. I passed those practical skills on to Alex as he began learning about life as a professional footballer. He had a perfect build for his preferred position in the back row – he stood almost 1.9 metres tall yet he was fast enough to play in the centres. He had a very professional approach to his footy and he was tough, so it was no surprise that Wayne Bennett thought very highly of Alex. But there was one thing I couldn't help him with – his room always looked like the scene of a bomb blast. Clothes and shoes were strewn everywhere. The carpet couldn't be seen. But Alex was clean around the rest of our place so he was a perfect housemate for me.

Alex was in love with a girl from his hometown. Teigan Power was like Alex in some ways – a young woman who seemed older than her teenage years. They were a great couple to be around, there was always plenty of laughter and good conversation. They had met at a party in 2010 and their relationship grew despite them living in different places. So, they had a bit in common with Kayla and me as we continued our relationship from different cities.

I had spent the final months of 2010 with Kayla on the Gold Coast, enjoying every day as our relationship grew. I knew I had to go back to Wollongong for pre-season training but I didn't want to go without Kayla. I had even cancelled an off-season trip to Las Vegas with a few mates so I could spend more time with her. I was desperate for Kayla to move to Wollongong and I must have sold it well because she agreed to move in January 2011, giving up a good job on the Gold Coast and regular contact with her family and friends to take a punt on life with me. Kayla and I both underestimated the challenges that lay ahead in our new life together. She had only moved to the Gold Coast in 2009, so she had done very well to establish herself in a new country in such a relatively short period of time. Now she was living in a new city, starting again from scratch, which was a big ask. But I would quickly learn that Kayla was never one to walk away from a challenge. Those next six months in Wollongong would be my first glimpse of Kayla's determination to achieve her goals.

She tried desperately to get work in Wollongong to build on the real estate career that she had started on the Gold Coast. That proved difficult, so Kayla began taking on temporary roles in Sydney, commuting each day. I could sense that Kayla was finding things challenging so I told her that she didn't need to work – we were comfortable enough to make ends meet. That shows how little I knew Kayla at the time. There was never any chance that Kayla wouldn't work. She ended up taking a job in a federal government call centre for a while, answering calls from victims of the floods that devastated Brisbane and beyond in early 2011. She was one of the most driven women I knew, which would become an important factor in our lives together.

Some people thought it was unusual that Kayla and I would share an apartment with Alex, but that's because they didn't know Alex. He was always such a good companion and he helped to make our place a real home. We were in an apartment across the road from the stadium in Wollongong – we were so close that we could hear the noise from the crowd. When Teigan came to visit, our apartment was always fun and noisy because we all got on so well.

Kayla and I had been together for months before we had our first argument, which was purely my fault. While I was desperately in love with Kayla, I hadn't told many people about our relationship. I wasn't on social media and I didn't talk about my life often, so our relationship wasn't widely known. I wasn't hiding it, I just wasn't someone who told people many things about myself. I should have told my manager George Mimis. He was a very important part of my life and I trusted George completely. That was the strange thing about my personality – I found it very difficult to trust people but, once I did, I trusted them without fail. So, when George rang me to say he had lined up a photo shoot and a positive article in a national magazine, I told him I would do it. I was never keen to do media interviews but George told me this was worthwhile, so that was fine by me. I didn't ask many questions, but George told me I had to go to Sydney for the photo shoot and, a few days later, a journalist would interview me over the phone.

The photo shoot wasn't what I had expected. They asked me to strip down to my underwear and then they took a series of photographs of me in all sorts of poses. That was unusual. I finished the photo shoot and headed home, unsure what I had just done. Copies of some of the photos were sent to me a few days later before the journalist rang for the interview. Kayla saw the photos and asked me what was going on. What magazine was I appearing in wearing nothing but underwear? I told Kayla that I didn't know the name of the magazine but a woman called Cleo was calling shortly to interview me. It was then that Kayla twigged to what was happening. She asked me if the magazine was called *Cleo* – the famous Australian publication for women. I told her that wasn't right – the reporter's name was Cleo. The reporter rang and it turned out her name wasn't Cleo, but she did work for *Cleo* magazine. And she thanked me for agreeing to feature in their 2011 Bachelor of the Year issue. Clearly, this was a difficult situation. The reporter then asked me what I looked for in a perfect woman. This wasn't going well, so I quickly ended the phone call.

Kayla was far from happy. She knew that my manager wouldn't line this up for me if he knew I had a serious girlfriend, so why hadn't I told George about her? She had moved her life from the Gold Coast to Wollongong and I hadn't told my manager about this? I didn't have an answer for Kayla so the conversation was short, but I struggled to get over the disagreement. I hated confrontation, especially with Kayla; I really disliked feeling sad and I felt that I had let her down badly. George, thankfully, convinced *Cleo* to take me out of the Bachelor of the Year edition, so that was a relief. But I took a few days to get over that argument. I didn't have the tools to cope when my emotions were tested like that, which was a sign of things to come.

I was pleased to have Alex in the apartment when the football season began with our trip to the United Kingdom for our World Club Challenge match against the reigning Super League champions Wigan Warriors. Alex wasn't in the squad so he stayed at home with Kayla. They got on well so I was relaxed about heading away for a match that we were keen to win. I found the World Club Challenge difficult because the English teams were a few weeks into their season, whereas we were in our pre-season, and we had to travel from the Australian summer into the northern winter. In 2011, we also had to contend with a loud Wigan crowd that got excited after the Warriors scored in the second minute. We twice recovered from deficits that night to win 21–15, taking the title of the best rugby league club team in the world.

We confirmed that title in the opening months of the NRL season as we charged to a 10–1 win–loss record. The premiership victory had not made us complacent, instead we were playing as well as any team I had played in during my career – even better than when we had won the 2010 grand final. Our confidence levels were extremely high, despite our opposition having the added incentive of playing the defending premiers – that was always something that seemed to motivate teams. We knew that we would be competitive in any match we turned up to play. That's the difference between good teams and bad teams – we didn't expect to win every game, but we expected to be a winning chance in every game. Good teams turn up every week knowing that they will play well rather than hoping that they will play well.

We were leading the competition despite constant speculation around Wayne Bennett's next move. Wayne was in the final year of his contract with the Dragons and he had made it known that he would coach elsewhere in 2012. Wayne had gone to Wollongong to win a premiership and he was looking for a new challenge. Journalists again linked me with Wayne's future, insisting we would go as a partnership to a third team. The prospect of Wayne going to Souths gained plenty of publicity in the media but it fell through, so I didn't give it much thought after that. Then Wayne told me that he had been approached by the Broncos and was strongly considering returning there. That was of great interest to me because I wanted to go back home. I had never wanted to leave the Broncos and I knew I wanted to finish my career there, so that was exciting. I still had my hopes up about that prospect when I learnt through the media after Round 5 that Wayne had signed with Newcastle for the next three seasons. I had not seen that coming, despite changes at the Knights occurring off the back of their new owner, mining millionaire Nathan Tinkler. Wayne reached out to see if I wanted to join him at the Knights, taking Kayla and me to dinner to discuss the move. I was interested but I told Wayne that there was one element that was non-negotiable – I had to be wanted by the club and not be considered a part of any deal with Wayne. I only wanted to go to a club that genuinely wanted me to play. Wayne told me that the Knights were very keen to get me there and that someone from the club would contact me.

While this was happening, the Dragons had tabled me another offer but I wasn't interested in staying there if Wayne wasn't around. The Dragons had been very good to me but, like Wayne, I was looking for a new challenge in 2012. Instead, I was keen to go to the Gold Coast Titans, because they were showing plenty of interest in me. The thought of going back to my hometown had extra incentive because it would mean Kayla could return to the Gold Coast and resume the life she had built for herself there. But there were financial worries around the Titans at the time, and that was a big concern. A good friend at the Titans had told me that they were concerned for their wages that season, so I needed to consider that. George Mimis also felt it wasn't the best career move, so he recommended that I look elsewhere. But I couldn't get the thought of returning to Queensland out of my mind and, while George told the Titans that I was going elsewhere, they sent a contract to my personal email, though I didn't feel great about going behind George's back because he had always been so good to me. I eventually decided to knock back the Titans' offer, which was fortunate because, if I had gone to the Gold Coast, I wouldn't have been going there to be a better player or a better person, which should have been my main reasons. It would have been a bad choice.

The Knights made contact with me and spelled out their hopes for the club under Wayne's direction and with the financial backing of Nathan Tinkler. The vision sounded solid, I liked the coastal location and I was happy to stay with Wayne. So, in the first week of June, I signed a four-year deal. The move would be refreshing, the club's potential was exciting and Kayla was happy to live in Newcastle. I was pleased to have that decision out of the way to enable me to focus on the rest of the football season. Alex also signed with the Knights, which for him meant heading closer to his hometown. I was rapt to hear that because the friendship between Alex, Teigan, Kayla and I was strong, and we were pleased for that to continue.

I had signed with Newcastle between the first and second State of Origin games for 2011. This was Darren Lockyer's last series and we were determined to win for him. After five consecutive series wins, our risk of complacency was overcome by the motivation to play well for Queenslanders who had been affected by the summer floods. I'll never forget the sight of the Suncorp Stadium playing surface filling with water at the height of the floods. For the rest of the 2011 season, teams played out of temporary change rooms at Suncorp Stadium while the flood damage in the usual rooms was repaired.

This Origin series again featured a bunch of my Dragons teammates, with Jamie Soward making his debut and earning plenty of media attention before Game I. He was joined in the Blues squad by Dragons Brett Morris, Mark Gasnier, Dean Young, Beau Scott, Ben Creagh and Trent Merrin. The Blues had five new players, but they took it to us under coach Ricky Stuart, overcoming a 10–0 deficit with tries in the sixty-fifth and sixty-ninth minutes to take the lead at Suncorp Stadium. That Queensland team thrived on close matches and we scored the winning try in the seventy-second minute when Johnathan Thurston and Darren Lockyer took advantage of a quick play-the-ball to find Billy Slater cutting back inside and dashing past the diving attempt of new Blues skipper Paul Gallen. That was a typically smart play from that trio – Paul had probably made fifty tackles already that night along with plenty of runs and he was being asked to race across to stop a charging Billy. It was a mismatch and it was good enough to get us the win.

The Blues beat us in Sydney in Game II, sending us back to the temporary change rooms of Suncorp Stadium for a decider that would be Locky's final match in a Maroon jersey. Locky admitted after the match that he was very nervous, realising that this would be the last of his thirty-six Origin matches. The team was also nervous but only because we were determined that Locky wouldn't leave without a win. It turned into a relatively comfortable night as we sped to a 24–0 lead after thirty-three minutes. But we had the misfortune of a serious knee injury to J.T. in the second half after he and teammate Ashley Harrison accidentally struck each other in a tackle. J.T. was taken from the field and re-emerged in a wheelchair to join our celebrations after the 34–24 win. It was a fitting farewell for Locky, who had made his Origin debut in 1998, when I was a ten-year-old watching from home.

The Origin series had a downside for me that year because it had a serious impact on the Dragons' season. With eight players involved in the series, we struggled to overcome the workload to settle back into the NRL season. In Round 20, we began a five-match losing streak that included two games when teams out of finals contention ran us down in the second half. The worst of those results was a collapse to South Sydney from a 20–0 lead after eighteen minutes. Wayne was exasperated and admitted in media conferences that he was out of ideas to rejuvenate us. After winning nine matches straight earlier in the season, we had to win our final two matches to avoid finishing in seventh place. It was a jarring end to the regular season and left us with limited confidence heading into the finals.

ABOVE: Lots of smiles in my early years … in a makeshift bath.

LEFT: Long hair, dodgy fashion sense. No wonder I wasn't smiling here.

BELOW LEFT: Christmas with Nana. I loved those early Christmas celebrations.

BELOW RIGHT: Athletics was a sporting love outside rugby league. In a relay at the state athletics championships in Brisbane.

ABOVE: A big smile with Nana and my grandfather Herbie.

RIGHT: Feeling good about my junior footy with one of the trophies that would take pride of place on a shelf in Nana's loungeroom.

ABOVE: I never let my uncle Dallyn get too far away from me. Here I am clinging to his leg with Nana and Mum.

LEFT: I really did adore my uncle Dallyn. He was always the joker. This picture was taken only a few years before his death.

ABOVE: The Under 11 South Coast representative team featured three of us who would play together for the Broncos – I'm third from left, Steve Michaels is in the black top in the middle and Denan Kemp is in front of him with the blue, white and black striped sleeves.

ABOVE RIGHT: It took a while … wearing my first Queensland jersey for the state schools team in 2005.

MIDDLE: Welcome to the NRL! Trying to tackle Cowboys legend Matt Bowen in my debut for the Broncos. Newspix.

RIGHT: Why wouldn't I be smiling? Twenty minutes into my State of Origin career and this was my second try. Newspix.

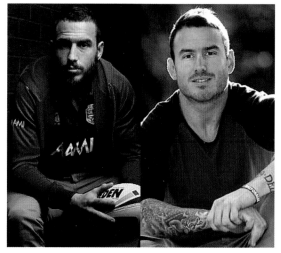

TOP: The breaking of the drought for Dragons fans. I celebrate our 2010 premiership, wearing the Clive Churchill Medal.

MIDDLE: Alex McKinnon doing what he does best – making others laugh. I'm in this photo with Macca and Wayne Bennett on my left, only a week before I went to the mental health clinic.

LEFT: A photo of me taken before I went into the clinic and one of me when I came home. The difference is obvious.

RIGHT: Kayla and me early in our relationship in 2011.

MIDDLE: Getting back from my Achilles injury was worth it. Celebrating a try in Origin I in 2015 with Greg Inglis, Billy Slater and Johnathan Thurston. Newspix.

BELOW LEFT: No wonder I'm smiling here, taking Willow on to the ground after a Test match in Perth.

BELOW RIGHT: Part of my captaincy duties for the Broncos – joining other NRL club captains in a promotional shoot before the start of the 2018 finals. Newspix.

TOP: Enjoying one of my favourite years in footy – running the ball back in the 2016 Origin series. AAP.

ABOVE: Rod Patison, my old high school coach, presented my 300th game jersey and Darren Lockyer presented Tom Dearden's debut; we were both PBC boys.

RIGHT: Triple century … a promotional photo shoot outside Suncorp Stadium as I prepared for my 300th NRL match.

With the three women I adore … Willow, Romi and Kayla.

I struggled during the last matches of the season as the losses took a toll. My life with Kayla was going well. We had a happy home that we continued to share with Macca who had made his first-grade debut in Round 14 that year, scoring twice in a loss to the Gold Coast Titans. Macca played in two other matches, making the most of the absence of our Origin players while showing the skills that had earned him such a big reputation among players across the league. I tried to be positive and fun around Kayla and Macca, but I was struggling to come to terms with our losing streak. Some of the older players in the team began to ask Wayne what was wrong with me. I would still be sulking on Monday or Tuesday at training. My body language showed that. I would be angry with myself for losing, particularly if I felt I didn't play well, and I wouldn't want to leave the house. I felt like I had to punish myself.

The regular season finished and we had reached a qualifying final against the Wests Tigers at the Olympic Stadium. The Tigers had won eight matches in a row while we were limping through August. We had plenty of chances to defeat the Tigers but fell 21–12, leaving us with a nervous wait to see if other results would go our way to keep our season alive. We survived for a sudden-death semifinal against the Broncos in Brisbane. This shaped up as Darren Lockyer's last game for the Broncos if they lost, ensuring plenty of publicity before the game. It was an epic match. We showed our strengths that night, digging deep with a brilliant defensive effort and then finding a try when everything seemed lost. We were down 12–6 in the seventy-eighth minute when the ball came my way and I was able to run around some tiring Broncos to score, earning plenty of boos from the Brisbane fans. Jamie Soward's outstanding conversion sent us to extra time. In the end, Locky would have the final say, kicking a wobbly but effective field goal to sink us 13–12 after just ninety seconds of extra time. What an effort by Locky – he was staring into the end of his career with his beloved Broncos yet he still found the ability to beat a rushing defence and put the game away. Full credit to the Broncos but I was very proud of the way the Dragons fought to the end when we weren't quite clicking on the field. It typified the determination that had delivered a premiership twelve months earlier.

That was the end of my Dragons career. I look back fondly on my time with one of the most successful clubs in Australian rugby league history. Most importantly, we helped to deliver a premiership for supporters who had waited a long time. I left my comfort zone to go to the Dragons and those three years helped me to grow as a person and a football player. But they also revealed more of the cracks that were opening in my life. When footy went well, so did life. When footy went badly, I began to struggle more and more away from the field. It was building up to a worrying point.

That was in the back of my mind as Kayla and I packed up to head to Newcastle, excited about the years ahead but unsure what they would bring us.

CHAPTER 9

Nathan Tinkler's Knights

I REALLY DIDN'T KNOW MUCH ABOUT NEWCASTLE WHEN I moved there late in 2011. I had played plenty of games there but I hadn't looked around the city much. There was a lot to like about it – the coastal location, its harbour, its people and the fact it wasn't as busy as Sydney, which was roughly two hours' drive south. Newcastle was a tough place to play for visiting teams because the Knights supporters always turned up. Even when the Knights were in the bottom four on the ladder, the club would be in the top four for home-crowd sizes. Newcastle was a proud rugby league town with a passion for the Knights, who had joined the league at the same time as the Broncos in 1988.

Before we arrived in Newcastle, Kayla and I bought a house in the coastal suburb of Fern Bay. Alex McKinnon had also signed with Newcastle, but he moved in elsewhere so Kayla and I lived together alone for the first time. Fortunately, Kayla took over the interior decorating, which meant that my collection of furniture, purchased without too much thought, was replaced with more appropriate choices. We were excited at the prospect of living together in Newcastle. Kayla, in her own determined way, set about making friends and looking for work in a new city.

After settling in, I had one job planned for as soon as possible – I wanted to ask Kayla to be my wife. That sounded easy in theory but the whole proposal was much harder in practice. Kayla and I had discussed getting married, so a proposal wouldn't come as a huge surprise, therefore the execution needed to be memorable. I made a plan that relied on Kayla being out of the house for a few hours so I could transform it for the proposal. When Kayla told me she had to go to Sydney, I knew this was my chance. Kayla would be gone for most of the day so I could get the house looking just as I wanted. That's when the troubles began. We only had one car, which Kayla was driving to Sydney, and I had to get to the shops to collect six huge balloons featuring the words 'Marry Me'. Unfortunately, the balloons were too big to fit into a normal taxi so I had to order a maxi taxi that would take me and the six balloons back home. And I did all this while standing on the side of a busy road in a rugby league town with my balloons. It wasn't ideal. I got the balloons home and placed them in our bedroom, tossing rose petals over the bed. I laid out extra rose petals and tea lights that made a trail from the front door of the house to our bedroom. I dressed in a suit, placed the engagement ring in my pocket and then waited for Kayla to come back from Sydney. I wanted to surprise her in the bedroom while on bended knee, ask her to marry me and, if she agreed, we would head out to a restaurant to celebrate.

I kept looking out the window, waiting to see Kayla drive up, so that I could rush into the bedroom and get in my will-you-marry-me pose. But Kayla had been held up in Sydney and, because she was unaware that I was proposing marriage, she wasn't rushing to get home. I couldn't do much about that so I waited and then waited some more. It was well and truly dark when Kayla finally arrived home, following the trail of tea lights and rose petals into the bedroom where she opened the door to find me on bended knee, hand outstretched asking: 'Will you marry me?' That's when Kayla began to laugh – it was a big laugh, too – at the sight of a guy not known for romance trying to pull off a very romantic move. This was more nerve-racking than any game of football. I found it much easier standing under a high ball in the final minute of a close match than I did proposing marriage. Fortunately, Kayla managed to say 'yes' amid the laughter, which at least lightened the mood. It was too late to go out for dinner but we celebrated at home. Proposal problems aside, I felt it was a perfect start to our lives in Newcastle. We decided to get married that year on 3 November, hopefully after a strong footy season with the Knights.

There were several reasons to be excited about the 2012 season for the Newcastle Knights. The club had reached the finals in 2011 under coach Rick Stone and our prospects looked healthy in the new season as Wayne Bennett came to town, looking for his twenty-first consecutive season in the finals. I was feeling the pressure of being the Knights' high-profile recruit. But the feeling I encountered in Newcastle from people I met seemed to be excitement as much as expectation. They were desperate for a good season. Since the Knights won the second of their two premierships in 2001, they had won one finals match. It had been a barren run for a team that had plenty of reasons to expect to play regular finals football.

The key figure at the Knights was mining magnate Nathan Tinkler – the former apprentice electrician who had turned an ambitious mining investment into a fortune apparently nudging $500 million. Nathan was a local guy who built a reputation as a generous helper to sports organisations that were doing it tough in the Newcastle region. His Hunter Sports Group purchased soccer's Newcastle Jets before taking over the Knights in March 2011. A good indication of how much Nathan was loved in the Hunter region was a vote of Knights' members on his takeover offer that received 97 per cent approval. When he signed Wayne to a four-year deal a few weeks later, even the 3 per cent of members who had voted against Nathan's takeover may have reconsidered. Nathan was rich, he loved his sport and he loved the limelight. He was big in every sense, from his physical build to his bank balance and his opinions.

My first meeting with Nathan was when he invited a bunch of Knights players and staff to his property outside Newcastle for lunch and a few beers. It was a pleasant afternoon and he seemed a nice guy on first impressions. When our long lunch finished, he invited us to join him in Newcastle for a night out. We jumped on a bus to head back into the city while Nathan jumped into his helicopter to meet us there. That's how he rolled.

His early weeks in charge in 2012 were characterised by generosity. We began the season with a much-hyped clash with the Dragons in Newcastle. My old team playing against a Knights team at the dawn of a new era. A massive crowd of almost 30 000 packed into Newcastle stadium for the match that was supposed to be the start of the Knights' journey towards a premiership under Wayne Bennett. The first steps were positive – we headed to a golden-point period after the scores were tied at 14–all after eighty minutes. In exactly the same way my previous NRL game ended, I was on the losing side as a field goal sank our hopes. Unlike my last game, the Dragons were the winners and Jamie Soward was celebrating after landing the match-winner.

It was a disappointing finish but that game had shown the Knights fans that our team had promise. The players' spirits lifted in the change room after the match when Nathan produced a wad of $2000 cash from his pocket to present to our player of the match. That was stunning – it just never happened at any other NRL club. Nathan promised us that win, lose or draw, and whether we played at home or away, the player of the match would receive $2000 from him. We would also be afforded a lavish after-match function, whether we were in Newcastle or away from home. Some NRL clubs were doing it tough but our team was owned by a millionaire who seemed unable to spend his money fast enough.

The first signs that something was wrong within the Tinkler empire came after our Round 6 win over the Eels at home. The $2000 payment for our player of the match was gone. And so was our grand post-match function. On an April night in Newcastle, following a win that left us in eighth place with a 3–3 win–loss record, we were suddenly like every other NRL team – no lump of cash for the best player and no luxury reception after the match. And no reason provided for the sudden change in plans. As the weeks went on, we began to learn more about Nathan Tinkler's personality. And it wasn't pretty. We built a 4–4 win–loss record before losing three consecutive matches to fall to thirteenth on the table. That tested the Newcastle fans who had expected a stroll to the finals in 2012 and then a run towards the grand final. Nathan was clearly among those fans because the losses were making him grumpy. We travelled to Brisbane for a Round 13 clash with the Broncos and Nathan invited the team out for dinner on Caxton Street the night before the game. He had clearly been drinking and that seemed to bring out grumpy Tinkler. At dinner, he started giving us his thoughts on the season so far. He asked me, in front of the team, whether I wanted some maroon sewn into the Knights jersey. According to Nathan I only played well for Queensland, so if he added a splash of maroon to the Knights jersey, would that make me play better for the team? I didn't answer the question but he moved on to Wayne, asking him why the Knights didn't sign Origin forward Nate Myles for 2012. 'I wanted him but you wouldn't pay the money,' Nathan said in a raised voice. His behaviour was as surprising as it was embarrassing, although Wayne handled him superbly.

His performance the next night would make that dinner conversation seem gentle. We had a terrible start to our match against the Broncos, falling behind 24–0 after only twenty minutes. At half-time, Nathan stormed into the change rooms and began shouting at players. He was almost frothing at the mouth and he wasn't holding back as he told us what he thought about our footballing skills. He did this while Wayne was making the long journey from the coaches' box down to the change rooms. He entered as Nathan was in full flight. Wayne didn't make a scene but he must have let him know what he thought of it all. Wayne made it clear with every team he worked for that he was the coach and he was to be allowed to coach in his way. He didn't appreciate interference. Nathan's behaviour was unacceptable that night although it fired us up because we stormed back to get within two points of the Broncos before they put their foot down and surged to a 50–24 win. We didn't hear a word from Nathan in the change rooms for the rest of the year.

Our season didn't improve when the Brisbane collapse was followed by a loss against Canberra, extending a five-match losing streak. That was not in the plans for Knights fans who had believed Nathan when he promised a top-four finish in 2012. After fourteen rounds, we had four wins and nine losses and sat in fourteenth place, a long way from his promised land. We recovered in the second half of the season, winning four out of five matches to take us into mid-August in ninth position with some chance of helping Wayne avoid his first year without finals football since 1991. But the fightback was tempered by increasing rumours about Nathan's financial problems. The rumours grew into a page-one story in the *Newcastle Herald* in August that claimed his companies had left a string of debts across the local region. The newspaper had spoken to business owners who said they were collectively owed more than $1 million from his Hunter Sports Group. With the aggression that his Knights players knew well, Nathan dismissed the rumours as a lie, claiming that all suppliers would be paid.

I knew how some of the business owners felt. I was owed money by the Knights. I had been paid my base wage each month along with the rest of my teammates but the other contract guarantees had not eventuated. The Hunter Sports Group continually told George Mimis and me not to worry – the money would all be paid; there had just been a few minor hitches that would be sorted out. That was a common response from Nathan and his spokesperson whenever questions about money were raised – nothing to worry about, all will be fine.

Nathan moved to Singapore in June that year but that was portrayed as a business decision so that he could apparently be closer to the Asian financial markets. We certainly played as though we were a team facing plenty of problems. We lost our last three games of the season. We came into the final match against South Sydney without any chance of making the finals but we still attracted more than 24 000 fans to our stadium. The game ended with a narrow loss against a top-four team, which was at least some consolation for Knights supporters.

Wayne had missed the finals for the first time since I was four years old. That meant that I had missed the finals for the first time in my career. As I had learnt, failure teaches you more than success. It was disappointing but it was a necessary step on a longer journey. The Knights fans let me know that they were unhappy with my performance that season. They pointed to the fact that I was among the highest-paid players in a team that was expected to make the finals, and I had scored only three tries that season – the first one coming in Round 21.

The only person more disappointed than the fans about my performance was me. Instead of owning my part in the Knights' season, I played the victim card. The bad habits that I developed at the Dragons had grown worse. If we lost a game on Friday night, I wouldn't leave the house that weekend. I felt that I had to punish myself for not performing well. I stayed home and sulked for most of our five-game losing streak. I wasn't handling the pressure that my high profile generated, accompanied by the ongoing discussion within the media and among Newcastle supporters that my form was letting the Knights down. For the first time in my career, I became obsessed with what was being said about me. I began to google my name, sometimes more than once a day.

The themes were similar – I was being paid a lot of money to play for the Knights and the team was losing; therefore, I was fair game for criticism. If a journalist wrote a negative article about me, I would simply refuse to have anything to do with them again. The anger and anxiety was growing within me and I was completely out of my depth in dealing with those feelings. I managed to hide the seriousness of my struggles from most people, including Wayne, but I couldn't hide it from Kayla. We had been together only two years and already I was showing her a worrying side to my personality. With Kayla's urging, I had begun to see a therapist in 2012 but that was too early for me. I wasn't in the right frame of mind because I kept blaming others for my problems.

Kayla was becoming frustrated by my behaviour, particularly my inability to help myself. I stumbled on, pretending that we were still ready to be married in November at Mission Beach in Far North Queensland. About a month before the wedding, Kayla and I had a long conversation in which she told me that our relationship shouldn't feel the way that it did. She was right, but I couldn't see that. I told her in a surly way that we should cancel the wedding if that was the way that she felt. But that was a step that I didn't want to take. Cancelling the wedding would have alerted my closest friends to my problems. I wasn't ready to tell my friends about those issues, so Kayla and I went to Mission Beach to be married on a steamy spring afternoon.

Kayla was the most stunning bride I had ever seen. I understood I was a very, very lucky man. The backdrop of tropical waters was perfect and we were rapt to have our closest friends and family in attendance. The event helped to paper over some of the issues that Kayla and I were becoming aware of in our relationship. I still experienced the weight of my family life as we looked after Nana, who had travelled north to be with us. I slept on the floor of Nana's room on the night before the wedding, helping to make sure that she felt fine. It was a huge trip for her; she was in her early eighties at that point. I hadn't spoken to Mum since 2005 and I wasn't about to invite her to the wedding. I would regret that in time.

Kayla and I headed off to Mexico for our honeymoon. We had promised in our vows to love each other despite whatever challenges would confront our marriage. We had no idea how soon those challenges would arrive and how seriously they would test us.

CHAPTER 10

Eight straight

My favourite State of Origin memory comes from my school days, watching Allan Langer carve up the Blues in the 2001 series decider. I was thirteen years old and as excited as any Maroons supporter when the bombshell dropped that Alfie had secretly returned from club football in England to play one final Origin match. Alfie helped us to regain the Origin shield only twelve months after we lost so badly in the famous 'grenade' game. A few Blues experts told the media that having Alfie return to play was a mistake by coach Wayne Bennett. But they're the odds that Queensland loves. Alfie scored a try and featured in another three tries as the Maroons thrashed the Blues at QEII Stadium in Brisbane.

I would build my own Origin memories in the twenty-eight matches I played for Queensland. But, after those games and our many series wins, Alfie's return was still my favourite. My excitement as a kid at his return had been replaced by awe. How the hell did he do it? I found that Origin was hard enough for younger players at their physical peak and used to the week-to-week swing of the NRL. Alfie had been gone from the NRL for more than two years, he travelled secretly from England to Brisbane, prepared himself at short notice and dominated the best players of the time only a few weeks short of his thirty-fifth birthday. It's a crazy thought and the memory of it has grown stronger for me in the years that have passed.

The margin for error in Origin matches is slimmer than in any football I have played. The teams have been so evenly matched over the years that mistakes can make the difference in any game. History shows how tight the competition is – from the first Origin game in 1980 until the end of the 2005 series nothing separated the teams. Queensland and New South Wales had each won thirty-six matches and there had been two draws. Then came the period of 2006 to 2013 when we won eight consecutive series. That sounds like a period of complete Queensland dominance and that's how it's often portrayed in media coverage. But that period was a lot tighter than many people might remember. We only recorded one clean sweep in that time and thirteen of the seventeen matches that we won were decided by ten points or less.

We were able to win most of the close games and that's what made the Queensland teams in that era so special. But winning them wasn't due to a single factor, like a high-tech edge that we had over the Blues. There was a combination of reasons that helped us blow open an Origin history that had swayed from state to state for twenty-five years and the reasons were simple: we kept the same team almost every year, drafting in new players when they were needed; our preparations for matches never really changed; we didn't sledge the Blues; and we ran the same plays. We had a play from a tap restart that we called Fourex. We added a few things to that play and it became known as Fourex Gold. We never strayed too far from the basics. We also kept our training relatively light. One year when I was at the Dragons, I compared our GPS data from Origin training sessions with Brett Morris, who was playing for the Blues. Brett had run twice the distance that I had run during training.

The most important reason for our eight consecutive series wins was the fact that we had a great team. And, as the years went on, we kept developing our combinations so we continued to improve. During many of our wins, we had Johnathan Thurston and Greg Inglis on one side of the field and Cooper Cronk and Billy Slater on the other. Between those edges, Cameron Smith touched the ball more than anyone. Cam, Coops, Billy and G.I. first started developing their combinations together at the Norths Devils in Brisbane before they played together for the Melbourne Storm. And, when they made their Origin debuts, they had the genius of Darren Lockyer to work off. Locky also played a strong role in J.T.'s emergence at Origin level. J.T. did things that even surprised his teammates. In Game II of the 2013 series, we were twenty metres out from the Blues' line when J.T. hit me on the chest with a pass that I barely saw coming. He had noticed in the blink of an eye that Blues winger Nathan

Merritt had sprinted in to jam his South Sydney teammate G.I., leaving me unmarked. Before I even noticed that Merritt had run in, J.T. had rifled a pass to me that couldn't have been better placed if it was from a set move that we had practised a hundred times. I caught the ball and scored a try. If we weren't expecting the pass, the Blues were always going to struggle to defend it.

We had forwards who were courageous in the way they laid the platform for the team. Our forwards had a mixture of size and style, but they formed a formidable pack. Smithy was the forward leader, using every advantage he could get for our team. That included a few conversations with referees that always fired up Blues fans. But Smithy was never out of line. He asked simple questions that often made the referee think about something in a way he may not have before. Smithy is unbelievably competitive without stepping over the line. And we had a support team of coaches and general staff who guarded the Queensland Origin spirit and ensured that it was passed on to the current generation.

The spirit was alive and well in 2012 when another decider went down to the final minutes. This time, it wasn't Locky or J.T. who knocked the Blues out – it was Cooper Cronk with a forty-metre field goal. The night before, Coops had stayed behind at training for half an hour to practise his field goals. He knew the game might be close so he wanted to make sure he had done enough practice if we needed a field goal to win the series. That was one of the reasons Coops, Smithy and Billy were so successful for so long together – they were professionals and always looked for any way they could improve themselves on or off the field. That included carefully watching their diets and the general maintenance of their bodies, and tweaking their training when needed. Coops was also a non-stop talker during games which was a great help to many of us, including J.T. who thrived with that level of communication.

Another advantage we had was that many of our clubmates played for the Blues. Before each game, we used to go over the strengths and weaknesses of each Blues player. The teammates of those players would lead the discussion. In 2011, seven of my Dragons teammates played for the Blues, including Jamie Soward on debut along with Mark Gasnier. I knew that Jamie loved to get early ball to Gaz so that he could do his thing. We tried that at the Dragons each week so I suspected it would be the same in Origin. In Game I of that series, I twice jammed Gaz and shut him down as the early ball from Jamie found him. It looked like well-planned defence but it was really just taking our club knowledge on to the Origin field.

Playing against clubmates, or former teammates, did not reduce the chance of a fight in Origin matches. The fans knew that they were more likely to see a fight during an Origin match than during club matches. Players seemed more on edge because of the tension that had built during the ten days in camp, combined with the atmosphere sparked by the huge crowds. There were plenty of scuffles during my Origin career but I was always on the edges of the action, grabbing a few jerseys. I wasn't a fighter so there was never any chance that I would be in the thick of it with our big men trading punches. Some players get motivated by a fight but it never interested me. I can't remember ever throwing a punch in any game I've played, going right back to my junior days.

My schedule on Origin days remained the same throughout my career. We would go for a team walk at about 10 a.m., which would include a game of cricket in a park. We would head back to the hotel to stretch before lunch at midday. I was never one to sleep on game day. It just wasn't my thing. In the afternoon, I would often catch up with Kayla or with friends for a coffee and then head back to the hotel for a snack at 4 p.m. We would do more stretching and then jump on the bus at about 5.30 p.m. to drive to the game. The big difference for Origin was that we couldn't warm up on the field before the game. That was an issue for wingers and fullbacks who liked to get on to the field and catch some high balls. The feeling in the Origin change room was also different from that in the sheds before a club game. For one, Alfie Langer would be more reserved in his role on our coaching staff. Before Broncos games, Alfie would be likely to crack a few jokes, which I always enjoyed, but Origin change rooms were quieter and players were left to prepare as they liked.

The home-ground advantage seemed greater in Origin games than in any type of football I played. I would feel much better if we had two games away from Sydney, even if one of those was in Melbourne. The Blues fed off the crowd's enthusiasm and they never seemed out of a game, even if we built a lead. That's why the 2013 series was such a big test for us. We had won seven consecutive series and we had to contend with a draw that included two matches in Sydney. We lost the opening game 14–6, and the Blues fans could sense a series win. One Sydney newspaper even wrote that Queensland was a 'shadow of its former self' in that opening match, while former Blues coach Phil Gould wrote that we were 'slow and laborious' and 'disorganised'. Mal Meninga reminded us about those comments as the series went on.

We came home for Game II and scored a try within the opening two minutes to get our crowd excited. We then cruised to a 24–0 lead in the second half – I scored two tries from J.T. passes – but a fight halted the game. Two players from each team were sin-binned, meaning G.I. moved to the left wing and I moved to the right wing for ten minutes as we reshuffled our team. That win set us up for a classic decider in Sydney while the fight gave Mal and our coaching staff some more ammunition to motivate us for an eighth consecutive series win.

Game III was an eighty-minute episode epitomising the determination, professionalism and pride of that Queensland team. The Blues fans had been waiting for this night – their chance to end the longest losing streak in Origin history with a decider at their home ground. But J.T. quietened them in the tenth minute with an individual try through a confused defensive line. We led 8–4 at half-time and then stretched to 12–8 when Justin Hodges scored on the right side. The crowd came to life in the seventieth minute when the Blues scored to narrow their deficit to 12–10. The final ten minutes made for an epic finale. And that's when the Blues really tried to use their home-crowd advantage. We had made a long run downfield with three minutes remaining and had the Blues completely cooked after a quick play-the-ball only a few metres out from the New South Wales line. But our certain try was in danger because a streaker had interrupted play, falling face down in front of the goalposts, five metres out from the tryline. Security guards swarmed on him while we planted the ball for a try to seal the series. But the try was sent to the video referee who ruled that the Blues' defence was obstructed by a naked bloke and some security guards. Fortunately, the interruption didn't matter as we completed a 12–10 win for an eighth consecutive series win.

That series was a fitting way to remember the Queensland team of that era: winning a decider in Sydney; overcoming a deafening Blues crowd; and proving wrong the critics who claimed that our best years were behind our team. I have fond memories of all of my Origin campaigns. I loved being in Origin camp and I loved the pressure of the big matches. They were an exciting time and, importantly for me, they removed me from my everyday life, particularly in 2012–13 as I really struggled away from the field. For ten days every few weeks in mid-winter, I escaped my real life and its growing problems. But it was always there, awaiting me when I returned.

CHAPTER 11

Rock bottom

MY LIVES ON AND OFF THE FIELD WERE A LONG WAY APART in 2013. The football was very good. The State of Origin series win was followed by the Knights storming into the preliminary final. And the Kangaroos finished the year winning the World Cup final in front of more than 70 000 people at Old Trafford. We were undefeated throughout the World Cup, crunching New Zealand 34–2 in the decider. I played on the wing in the final, marking Roger Tuivasa-Sheck for only a few minutes before he was injured and taken from the field. The win was one of the most comprehensive victories of my international career and it meant a lot to the five players who had lost to the Kiwis in the previous World Cup final in 2008.

My selection for the World Cup came after a much better season for the Knights. The disappointment of 2012 was followed by some important developments: we gained experience, with nine players aged over thirty; Wayne Bennett was more familiar with the squad; and the players were more familiar with Wayne. But some mixed form during the season meant that we still had to win our last two matches to qualify for the finals, including a trip to Brisbane to beat the Broncos. We then thrashed Parramatta by 48 points in the last round, bringing good form into our opening finals match against Canterbury. We won that game 22–6, sending us to Melbourne to take on the Storm in a sudden-death final. We were rank outsiders against a Storm team that specialised in finals footy, especially against teams like us that had fluctuated through the season to finish seventh. Yet we were never headed that night, skipping to an 18–4 lead before a desperate Storm fought back. It was one of the most memorable wins of my career simply because most people did not expect it. There is an upside when nobody thinks that you can win – there is no pressure. We still wanted to win, but we went out to enjoy ourselves and to play well. The Storm were trying to live up to huge expectations. There would be no prospect of an honourable defeat for them. We could lose honourably and still impress most of our fans who were proud of the way we had cruised through the first week of the finals. But we came away with a win that Knights fans could cherish.

We were confident we could continue our run in the preliminary final against the Sydney Roosters, but we struggled after Danny Buderus was knocked out in the opening minutes. We needed things to go our way that night and Danny's loss was critical to our chances. We didn't recover and the Roosters went through to the grand final. We were proud to make the final four, which was Newcastle's best result since 2001, increasing the expectation for Knights supporters for the following year. They remained hopeful that Wayne would take us to a premiership in the same way he broke a drought for the Dragons.

But the 2014 season never got off the ground for the Knights. There were more than a few frustrated players as we entered the new season. I was still owed money from my contracts in 2012 and 2013. Every time I asked about the outstanding money, I was told everything would be paid. But that was starting to look less likely as the Knights began to hit serious financial problems stemming from the failure of Nathan Tinkler's company to pay bills. The catering company that provided lunch for the players a few times each week refused to bring any more food until it received all outstanding debts. As a result, our team nutritionist would go to the supermarket and buy some hot chickens to be shared among players for lunch. We were also sharing sports drinks and protein shakes as funds became too tight to get the basics that other clubs enjoyed. Worse was to come as we realised that some players had not been paid superannuation for twelve months. Our pay slips indicated that superannuation had been paid but the money had never gone into our accounts.

The rumours about Nathan Tinkler had grown over the past eighteen months, despite his usual claim that he was simply the victim of a media campaign. In November 2012, only days after Nathan had again blamed the media, the trainer of his massive horse-racing empire admitted that he had gone weeks without vets and farriers and had run out of feed for the horses at times because of a lack of money. So, it wasn't surprising that the money problems were seriously affecting the Knights. The club at least had the benefit of its monthly grant from the NRL, which was always slightly more than the monthly salaries for players. That grant arrangement gave players the confidence that we would be paid, with the Knights depositing our salaries on the fifteenth day of each month. In early 2014, our football manager advised us that there was some concern that we wouldn't be paid according to our schedule. He warned us to get in touch with our banks if we had any direct debits set up in the days after the fifteenth of the month – he thought it would be wise to put any automatic debits on hold. That wasn't a great time for our squad. The players were being asked to put their bodies on the line for a millionaire owner whose companies didn't pay their bills. While we were all professionals and wanted to win, it wasn't a great incentive for teams to play well.

When it came time for the 2014 season launch, I let Wayne know that I wouldn't be there because I had a wedding to attend for one of Kayla's friends in New Zealand. Wayne was fine with that, telling me that he was happy for me to go to the wedding. The problem was that the media didn't know I was away so they arrived at the season launch and made a note of my absence, asking if it was a sign of disharmony in the club. Nathan also didn't know – and he was far from happy. He rang my mobile phone while I was in New Zealand and left a message that could have melted the phone. The message included the following words: 'Who do you think you are? How dare you not come tonight. You are supposed to be here. I will crush you. You are nothing.' On it went. It was the best spray I had ever copped. I didn't worry about calling back – I had never gone looking for confrontation and I didn't feel in the mood to take another character assessment from an angry millionaire whose companies didn't pay their bills. But the next time I saw him, it was like nothing had happened. The man who promised to crush me greeted me as a friend. I didn't raise the matter with him – I couldn't be bothered lighting his short fuse. That was life with Nathan Tinkler as a football club owner. In the end, the failure of his companies to pay bills caught up with him. The NRL took interim ownership of the Knights in June after the players had not been paid. At the same time, Nathan announced that he was finished with owning sports teams. That was a good outcome for everyone.

The NRL took over the Knights when our season was all but done with a 2–11 win–loss record that had us in last place. The season had never really begun for us after new recruit Russell Packer was jailed over summer for assault. Our playmaker Jarrod Mullen was injured in the pre-season. Only ten minutes into the first game of the season, I strained my hamstring which ruled me out for several weeks. Things weren't going well on the field, which meant that they weren't going well off the field for me. The clouds were closing around me and I had no clue how to lift them.

Kayla was the only person who knew how much I was struggling off the field. It wasn't easy to hide it from my teammates but it was impossible to hide it from my wife. That was unfair for Kayla because she was enjoying Newcastle. She opened a dress shop in the city in 2013 and she began to make some good friends. Kayla liked the strong community feel of Newcastle, especially the friendships that she had made. And they would be extremely important for Kayla in the coming years. Meanwhile, I was in Newcastle with the wrong mindset. I mistakenly believed that there was only one reason I was in the city – to play football. And, when we lost games, I would wonder why I was there. That's how little I knew about life.

My selfishness extended to my behaviour in our marriage. I did whatever I wanted to do, whenever I wanted to do it. I would come home from training, I would eat and I would play computer games. I wasn't looking to learn much about life. If Kayla's friends came over to our house, I barely gave them the time of day. I would continue to play computer games, which was disrespectful to Kayla and embarrassing for her. I was immature and naïve. I didn't know how to be a husband. That's not an excuse – it's an observation of my behaviour at the time. I didn't have the tools to deal with my worsening situation and I didn't have anyone who I felt like seeking advice from. I had people around me like Wayne who could help me, but I never asked them. If I couldn't handle losses in footy, how was I going to handle life? I wasn't likely to get much help within footy in 2014 because the game then didn't focus on welfare. If a player wasn't his usual self, no one really checked in and asked how things were going.

But that welfare focus changed forever after Newcastle's Round 3 match against the Storm on a Monday night in Melbourne. I missed that game because of my hamstring injury, instead watching at home with Kayla. The game was forty seconds from half-time when Alex McKinnon took the ball in Melbourne's half and charged upfield the way he had done so many times. He stepped off his left foot and straightened towards a group of three Melbourne defenders. Macca was lifted in the tackle and driven dangerously towards the turf, landing on his neck in the most awkward fashion. I had a bad feeling about the tackle immediately. It wasn't so much that Macca had been tipped too far – plenty of players had gone further above the horizontal – but it was the way in which his neck took all the force of impact. My concern grew with the length of time it took for Macca to be treated and taken from the field. Plenty of players get hurt in our game but not many are treated with the caution and care that Macca received that night. There was clearly something wrong. Kayla immediately sent a text message to Teigan to tell her that we were thinking of her and hoping that Macca would be fine. I knew that he had been hurt but I fully expected that Macca would be back playing footy again in 2014 – isn't that what happened for most people in our game who were injured? But Teigan's phone call to Kayla later that night only increased everyone's fears – Macca had injured his C4 and C5 vertebrae and there was real concern that the injury could be extremely serious.

By the Tuesday, doctors had confirmed the devastating news – Macca had suffered a severe spinal injury. We would learn that Macca may never walk again and his career was over after forty-nine NRL matches. Macca would have played State of Origin for New South Wales. He would have played for at least a decade in the NRL. He would have been the heart and soul of any great NRL club. He was a player who had become a complete professional in only a few years without ever losing the personality for which he was so loved. Macca was twenty-two years old and he may never walk again.

The injury hit Kayla and me particularly hard because Macca and Teigan had become our closest friends in Wollongong and Newcastle. The friendship that Macca and I had started four years earlier had become the closest friendship I had known. I always felt a different person when I was around him and I knew that he made me a better person. That would sink in over time. We didn't see Macca until he was moved from Melbourne to a Sydney hospital where he continued his recovery. It wasn't until I visited him in Sydney that I really began to grasp the extent of his injury. My old flatmate – a young man who always made me feel at ease and was genuinely interested in my life – was facing a huge battle. But there he was in his hospital bed with that unmistakeable Alex McKinnon grin. He was in good spirits, more interested in what was happening in my life and around the Knights than he was in my questions about his health. Macca's life had been devastated but he was still smiling. His courage and his attitude were inspiring. Macca is an incredible bloke.

As I drove home from Sydney, I pulled over to the side of the road and cried. I was devastated for him but I was also angry at myself. Macca was smiling and he knew that he may never walk again let alone play rugby league. I could walk and I could play football, yet I was angry and anxious. I struggled to reconcile that. I was turning myself into the victim because I was battling in my life and I was unable to cope with any losses. I certainly wasn't a victim but I couldn't train my mind to think any other way. I began to rarely leave home except for training, playing or seeing Macca. I didn't want to go outside and I didn't want to hang out with any of my teammates. I was starting to feel real pain and I had no idea how to cope with that.

The Knights won two of our three games after Macca's injury before we went on a seven-game losing streak that would sink my time at the club. This was a terrible stretch for the team and for me. After a loss, I would go home and not leave the house for days unless I had to go to training. I'd be the last person to get to training and I would be the first person to leave, heading straight back to my house. I wouldn't go anywhere else. I was short with Kayla and I took no interest in anything that she did. I was so grumpy that I made Kayla feel as though she was walking on eggshells every day.

But I could always look forward to the oasis of the State of Origin camp. This was the best and worst thing that could happen to me. It was the best from the viewpoint that Origin camp was my favourite time of the year – I was in an environment that I loved, around people who I liked and playing in one of the most anticipated sporting competitions each year. But it was the worst because Origin camp only put my problems on hold and further damaged my marriage. When I joined the Origin camp in 2014, I went a week without speaking to Kayla. I pretended I had no problems, so I wasn't about to ring home to remind myself that my world was really in trouble. I didn't get the result I had hoped for on the field as Queensland lost its first Origin series since 2005. Cooper Cronk broke his arm in the first ten minutes of Game I and the Blues won the opening two matches to finally reclaim the Origin shield.

I went into camp for the third match and again buried my head, forgetting about life at home. But Kayla rang me one night early in the camp to tell me that she had had enough, that this wasn't how a marriage should feel. She was leaving me. She said she would move out the next day and not be there when I returned from Origin camp. Kayla told me she couldn't help me anymore and that I needed to seek professional help. The real indication that I wasn't mentally well was the fact that Kayla's announcement barely troubled me. I was in Origin camp so how could I be worried about anything in the outside world? The other indication came in my performance in the final Origin match. I played well and we thrashed the Blues with four tries in the second half.

I walked out of the Maroons' team hotel the next morning to head to the airport and back to my new home life when I was met by a television reporter who wanted to interview me about the Origin game. Her request was reasonable and it would have taken me about two minutes to stand there and politely answer her questions. Instead, I kept walking and answered her questions in a way that swung between impolite and plain rude. The camera was filming as I did this, which meant that I was building up a new interview to rival my disaster from when I was with the Dragons five years earlier. The interview went viral that day, earning me plenty of criticism from the public and laughter and support from other NRL players.

I came home to Newcastle to find our house mostly empty. Kayla had moved her furniture into storage and she had found another place to live. At her dress boutique, Kayla had given the landlord notice that she would be packing up the shop in the coming weeks and leaving Newcastle. This was no threat from Kayla – she was starting a new life without me. It took me a few days on my own at home before I started to really struggle. I began to think about my life and what I had – or didn't have. I had no family. I hadn't seen Mum for years. Nana was in a nursing home and her health was beginning to fail. I didn't have many really close friends. And my wife was now gone. I tried to contact Kayla to ask her to meet up with me but she was getting on with her own life. I had treated her so badly for so long, why would she do me any favours?

I played another two matches for the Knights, including the Round 19 home match against the Titans. This was the 'Rise For Alex' round across the NRL, honouring Macca for his bravery and his inspiring attitude and to raise money for his ongoing medical costs. Macca joined both teams on the field before the match, sitting in his wheelchair and taking in one of the most emotional moments I have been involved with in football. The crowd roared for Macca and then chanted 'Alex, Alex, Alex' and 'Newcastle, Newcastle, Newcastle'. There was a feeling in the stadium that day that was hard to describe. We wanted to win this game as a sign of the respect we held for a man who had started the season playing alongside us. The Knights had won their last three matches and, while a finals spot was out of reach, we were still expected to play well. However, we were our own enemies that day, making too many errors as the Titans won 22–6. That was a gutting result because we felt like we had let Macca down. I wasn't able to support him in the way that he needed a friend to support him, so playing well and winning for him were the next best things. Macca was in the change rooms after the game and, as always, was smiling. When didn't he smile? He was incredible.

At the same time, I had never been angrier. I had looked back at some photos of me as a child and I always had a big smile on my face. There I was at my grandparents' house or with my uncle Dallyn laughing. That smile was gone. I rarely looked people in the eye anymore – I preferred to look at the ground.

I was confused. Why was I angry? Why did I act the way I did? Why did I close myself off to life in general? Looking back on it, the answers went to the core of my life. The two father figures in my life – my uncle Dallyn and grandfather Herbie – had died when I was young. I believed that Mum had abandoned me, deciding she no longer wanted to be part of my life. And Nana's health was in serious decline, meaning the woman who had meant so much to my formative years now needed daily care. Every member of my small family had been taken away from me in some form. If it came to a Boyd family Christmas lunch, there was no one really left to sit with me at the table. I was trying to start a new life with Kayla but I didn't know how to love her the way that a husband should love his wife.

The loss of those family members had damaged my ability to trust. If things that you loved were always to be lost, what was the point? My reputation for being rude and cold in media interviews came from that trust problem. It wasn't that I didn't want to talk about my life, I just didn't trust journalists to tell it the way that I felt it needed to be told. So I shut myself off and made a fool of myself in the eyes of some people. If I couldn't build an ability to trust people, how was I going to make my way through life?

After the Rise For Alex match, I did my usual stay-at-home thing through Sunday night and into Tuesday. This time, I realised that it was different. I had reached breaking point. I couldn't deal with this on my own anymore. I needed help. I rang Kayla and asked if I could see her. Kayla was renting an apartment and was on the way to regaining the independence and determination that had attracted me to her when we first met. She agreed to let me come over that Tuesday night but it was clear that she was reluctant to have me in her new place. When I arrived, Kayla told me that it appeared I had lost weight and that I wasn't looking well. I fought back tears as I told Kayla that I was struggling. I had no idea what was wrong but I knew I was in pain and I needed it to go away. The pain had become so great that I realised I just couldn't deal with it – I needed help. And the biggest sign of danger was this – I didn't want to play football anymore. I meant it. I was done. I had lost my love for the one thing that had been a constant in my life since childhood. It had been my escape for so long, but my troubles had become overwhelming and there was no place I could now hide. I then sobbed uncontrollably.

Kayla was calm and caring. She suggested that I needed professional help and I needed it quickly. Just like a serious physical injury that needed attention, my mental health now required expert assistance. But who could point me in the right direction at this time of night? I composed myself enough to call George Mimis, who had always been a great help as my manager and a genuine friend to me. If anyone would know, it was George. I broke down again on the phone as I told him for the first time the depth of my troubles. George quickly arranged for Jan Earl, a nurse from a mental health clinic in western Sydney, to call me. I took Jan's call and immediately found a connection with her. Jan, whose son, Sandor Earl, was an NRL player, organised for me to move into her clinic for a rehabilitation stay. I would put my football season on hold and seek help. Within an hour of arriving at Kayla's place, I had gone from being a blubbering mess to booking a stay at a mental health clinic. They would be among the most important hours of my life.

That decision brought me instant relief. The next day, Wednesday, 23 July 2014, I drove from Newcastle to western

Sydney to check into the clinic for a 21-day program. I rang Wayne and told him about my decision. He was extremely supportive and asked me how I wanted to handle it with the club and the media. Wayne asked whether I wanted to say that I was injured if that would help me cope with it. From a certain viewpoint, I was injured, but I was done running away from my problems so I told Wayne to advise the Knights that I was going in for mental health treatment. I didn't care if the media knew about it. I said that I would miss some games but I would be back to finish the season. That's how naïve I was when it came to understanding how much help I needed.

I arrived at the clinic and, at first sight, it was a bit daunting. All I knew about rehabilitation clinics were stories about the locations where celebrities would go to seek help. They sounded more like resorts than mental health clinics. In the middle of winter, the place I pulled up at didn't look warm, modern or inviting. But it was just what I needed. Jan met me in the foyer and began the task of settling me in to the clinic that would be my temporary home for the next three weeks. I was taken to my room which was small and plain but had all I needed. There was a bed, bathroom and television. The rules were simple: I couldn't leave the facility for the first three days and I couldn't have visitors in that time. After three days, I could have visitors and I could leave for up to an hour for basic tasks such as visiting the shops. I was welcome to go anywhere between my room and the common areas of the clinic. I could stay in my room the whole time if I wanted to, but that wasn't recommended. I had to wait until 4 p.m. each day to use the gym – it wasn't the most expansive gym but it was good enough for what I needed. I would receive three meals a day, which I could choose to eat in my room or in the dining room. And I could use the communal loungeroom, which had cable television so there was access to every NRL match if I wanted to watch them. For the next three weeks, this was my weekday schedule:

7 a.m.: Breakfast

9 a.m.: Group session

11 a.m.: Group session

Noon: Lunch

1 p.m.: Group session

3 p.m.: Individual therapy session

4 p.m.: Gym session

6 p.m.: Dinner

Jan was a great listener. She had a real ability to cut to the core of my problems. During my introduction to the clinic, Jan arranged for me to see a psychiatrist. This assessment would give some insights into the pain I was feeling. After speaking to the psychiatrist, I was told that I was dealing with adjustment disorder, most likely stemming from stress during my youth. Adjustment disorder relates to a change in a life situation that causes a stressful reaction. I was told that adjustment disorder could spark feelings of depression, anxiety, social isolation and unusual behaviour. I could tick off all of those symptoms. They had become my life. The psychiatrist and Jan recommended that I attend cognitive behaviour therapy groups.

The group sessions were optional but Jan encouraged me to attend and I was glad I did. They included a mixture of about fifteen to twenty people – women, men, older, younger, some battling drugs and alcohol, others eating disorders, depression and anxiety. We were all there together and we all wanted to get better. I didn't say much in the first two group sessions – I was happy to sit back and take it in. Two guys in the group recognised me which wasn't a surprise. Exactly three weeks earlier, I had been playing State of Origin, which was the highest-rating television show in the country. It wasn't like I could go in there and expect my identity to go unnoticed among group members. The Knights had already issued a media release that confirmed I was stepping away from the game for mental health reasons so my absence wasn't a secret.

The group sessions covered different topics to equip us with tools to improve our lives – how to find gratitude, how to solve problems and set goals. We did art therapy and yoga. After a few group sessions, the facilitators began to ask me questions to get me involved. I enjoyed contributing even though speaking before a group of people I barely knew was something I usually avoided. The best thing about the group sessions was realising that you were not alone. Some people seemed to be really struggling in their lives. I could see their pain and desperation. I felt for them because I learnt that, while we were all in it together, some people had long roads to travel to overcome their pain and they had been trying for years to do that.

I began receiving visits towards the end of my first week. I was very grateful to those who came to visit me – Kayla, Wayne, George, Wendell Sailor and Greg Inglis. I know Macca would have been there if he could, but it was impossible for him at that stage. Each of those people brought me something different. I will never forget their generosity in taking an interest at that time. Wayne told me that he noticed a difference in me immediately. Kayla said that I was already starting to look healthier – she had been shaken by my appearance when I went to her apartment on the night before checking into the clinic. She found the visit difficult because she considered that we were still apart. Kayla had endured a lot from me over recent years and she wasn't ready to resume our marriage yet. I had to accept that, all the while hoping that she and I would get back together. Wendell brought his good humour, which was what I needed, while G.I. and I had formed a bond over many years as Origin roommates and teammates. His friendship was always valued.

The gym sessions were a highlight of my day. For ninety minutes I was able to do some exercise that helped with my rehabilitation. Exercise is such an important part of good mental health and that was available to me within a routine that I enjoyed. I had all of my meals in my room and would watch television before going to sleep. The nights and weekends were the most difficult times – that was when you had to work harder to keep the negative thoughts out. So I found myself often watching television in the communal room, even watching some NRL matches, including Knights games.

When I watched those matches, I realised that I wasn't missing footy. It had become part of my problem – the expectation, the losses, the criticism, the fans, the media. I didn't know how to deal with it all and I was now learning tools to help me cope when I returned to the game. That return wasn't going to happen in 2014. I still expected that but it became clear in my time at the clinic that I wouldn't be playing again that year.

I was told that I needed to focus on three things: to take a break from football; to reconnect with my mum; and to make my relationship with Kayla my priority. They were my three most important goals. Jan told me that I needed a plan for my life outside the clinic. It was easy to go to the clinic, but it was harder to return to the outside world and cope with its challenges. I knew the risk: going back to footy immediately meant going back to the troubles that I had come from. The Knights had four matches remaining – three at home and one in Brisbane. When Jan urged me not to return to rugby league in 2014, I knew that she was right. It would be a trap and I didn't need that after the progress I had made at the clinic. I let Wayne know that I wouldn't be back for the rest of the season. He was great about it, as I expected. I felt bad for my teammates at the Knights and for supporters because I wasn't returning in 2014. It didn't sit well with me but I had to make the best decisions for my personal situation at that time. It wasn't easy to do because I always felt a sense of duty to my club, but Jan was clear that I needed a break. It was the right decision.

I also had another decision to make – where would I play in 2015? In the same week that I checked into the clinic, Wayne had shocked the footy world again by announcing that he was returning to the Broncos as coach for the next three seasons. Wayne had negotiated an early end to his Knights contract after all of the troubles in the Tinkler era. I knew immediately that I wouldn't be staying at Newcastle the following year, even though I had one year to run on my contract. With Wayne going and my mental health struggles, I needed a new city. I had no idea where I would play.

But for now I was able to push those concerns down the track. I had more urgent things to consider relating to how I could make myself better. Jan had summed up my problems in her expert way. She told me that she had seen many examples of how poor emotional attachment as a child had led to lifelong problems. That emotional attachment stemmed from my relationship with Mum, particularly as she battled her mental health issues and left our home to seek treatment. That had created the major adjustment issue in my life that I had been unable to cope with for so many years. Jan explained that my relationship with my mother was one of the many 'open doors' in my life that had to be closed. I could only close that door by seeing my mum again. The issue of my father's identity was also an open door, but that door may never be closed, even by learning my father's name. And if I never knew that, then I would have to close that door some other way.

The other open door was my marriage with Kayla. And that door was wide open. I wanted our marriage to work more than anything, but Jan told me that I had never been given a good example of how to love within a marriage so I had been trying to find my way while also dealing with adjustment disorder. Clearly, I wasn't doing a great job of that. When I closed those important doors, I could be a better friend to the likes of Macca.

To make it all work, Jan told me I needed to 'flourish' as a man. I was in the critical age group of twenty-four to twenty-eight when a man's mindset is being cemented, for better or for worse. I had to take control and make my mindset work for me. I didn't need medication to do this. I had gone to the clinic with an open mind about my treatment, but it was decided that coping strategies rather than medication were my best way forward.

The first move was to stay away from rugby league for the rest of the season. To help realise my goals, I had a list of things to concentrate on: I had to be grateful; I had to be resilient; and I had to avoid getting worked up about the small things in life. Jan urged me to consider becoming a mental health ambassador. Her many years working with people like me had convinced her that there weren't enough well-known people telling stories about their experiences. She told me that I could do a lot of good in this area and it was something that I began thinking about. I was encouraged to begin a journal, writing down my thoughts as a way to track my progress. I would write down the many things that I should be grateful for, reinforcing all of the positive parts of my life. Before I left the clinic, I went to the shops and bought a small journal with a brown cover. I scribbled the following words across the first page of the book:

MY THOUGHTS.

MY FEELINGS.

MY LIFE.

Start August 2014!

I decided to go on an overseas holiday as soon as I left the clinic, to help me get away from any temptations while the NRL season continued and to help me focus on my relationship with Kayla. I was fortunate to be able to take time off and to be able to afford to travel to Europe for a few weeks. It would provide me with the first opportunity to begin 'closing' my open doors: I wanted Kayla to come with me, although I knew that was a huge ask. Kayla wasn't ready to re-commit to our marriage but she agreed to come overseas with me as long as I understood her thinking.

The last thing I did before leaving the clinic was write a plan for my next steps in my journal which included reminders to smile, enjoy life, do charity work and try new things. Before I wrote my first journal entry, I filled up another page:

GREATFUL FOR:

Beautiful, loving, caring wife!

Fit, healthy body!

Great career!

Paid well!

Live in a great country!

2 awesome dogs!

A few close support people!

A few close friends!

Looking back at the opening pages of that journal, I notice that I couldn't spell grateful. That's how little I knew about gratitude. I couldn't spell it even though I had always been good at spelling. It was a sign that I had so much to learn, but at least I had taken the first steps. The three weeks that I spent at the clinic, where I had the support of so many people, was a huge turning point in my life. I knew that I had many reasons to be grateful. Now I had to go out and live that new life.

CHAPTER 12

After the clinic

LAZING IN THE GREEK SUN, LOOKING OUT OVER THE Mediterranean Sea without any pressing deadlines. Surely life didn't get much better than that? Not quite. Jan Earl was right – the rehabilitation journey wasn't easy, even when the surroundings were good enough for a postcard. Jan told me that the hardest part of my rehabilitation would start the moment I walked out the door of the clinic. That's why I headed overseas, because I knew I wasn't ready to go back to my old surrounds. It meant that I missed Macca and Teigan's engagement party – a really bright moment for two great people. I was rapt for them but I had to make sacrifices to make sure I kept improving. But life wasn't easy.

Journal entry
Saturday, 13 September 2014
One month after leaving the clinic

I don't know how I got to this point. Sometimes I feel so low
I feel like I don't deserve anything good or any happiness
in my life! I feel guilty about so many things and it's hard to
let go. I feel guilty that I pretty much forced Kayla to come
on this trip. I pushed her away so many times and when she
finally left I couldn't handle it. She was happy when she left
and again, thinking about myself, I begged and begged her
to give me a chance and come on this trip. At some stage
in my life I need to grow up, be a man and deal with what
I have created and face the outcome of the situation – just
deal with it! Not run away, beg and make people do things
they don't want to do. Nothing is going to change for me
until I change. It's obviously hard because I can't start the
new beginnings in my life until we are at home. Once I start
those things I know I'll be on the right track. As for me and
Kayla, it's very hard. To have a chance, I know she wants
me to show that I can take control more, organise things
and generally get things done. I want her to be happy.
I want her to know none of this is her fault. I want her to be
able to do whatever she strives for and I'll support her. She
deserves that regardless of whether we are together or not.
In the meantime, I need to remember the bigger picture.
I've had a lot of positives this past month since I went to
rehab. I have a plan that is going to better me. I just have to
enjoy the last week of the trip.

Some days were better than others, but none of them were
nearly as bad as before I went to the clinic. I had been given

tools – I just had to learn how to use them. My first major test came when a story broke in Newcastle accusing me of disloyalty. The media got hold of a photo Kayla posted on social media showing us enjoying Greece. The story made one blunt suggestion – I wasn't really that 'depressed' given the photo of us on holiday while, back at home, the Knights' poor season was ending. I can see how it was a bad look – I can understand how Knights fans would not have been impressed. But that story opened my eyes to two things: how a social media post can create a news story and the lack of understanding within media about the challenges of mental health. The story claimed that I hadn't informed the Knights of my plans. In fact, the Knights knew where I was and how long I would be away. I hadn't told the club boss, but I had told Wayne and I knew that George had clearly informed the club of my plans. Of course, I didn't want to be away but I had one chance to do what was best for my long-term future and I was taking that opportunity. I had put footy first my whole life and now I had to look after myself.

The story broke after we had left Greece for England to visit my former Broncos teammate Joel Moon and his family. I relished that part of the trip, seeing one of my oldest mates as a husband and father and taking his responsibilities in life seriously. I needed to see examples of good families living together because I had such little experience of that. The trip was helpful for my rehabilitation but it wasn't going well in my quest to close one of those 'open doors' that the clinic had helped me to identify. Kayla and I were finding it a real challenge to work through the struggles of our relationship. And that was before we returned to Australia to resume our normal lives, whatever that would look like. Kayla planned to find a place to live in Sydney, which would become her new home. I still didn't have a club for 2015 – the Broncos were my preference but there was a long way to go before I could confirm anything. The fact that Kayla would be living in Sydney made me interested in offers from Sydney clubs, though I didn't know where I would be living or whether Kayla and I would be together. That was scary, but I had to remember the tools I had been taught at the clinic if I was to get through it.

Journal entry

Sunday, 21 September 2014

It's our last night away. Overall, the trip has been positive and worth doing. Back to reality soon. I'm looking forward to it because I know I still need a lot of help in some areas but I also have things I need to do. I have written a list of those things which I need to start getting done or at least put them in place. I need to see George so we can get a few things sorted, mainly what I'll be doing next year. I have been really positive this last week. I've been thinking 'what will be, will be' and I know that, whatever happens, I'll be able to handle it. (I HOPE!!)

The 'open door' that needed closing as soon as I returned home was reuniting with Mum. It was critical to my rehabilitation journey. There was one problem – I didn't know where Mum lived or how to contact her. I knew that she was somewhere on the Gold Coast but I hadn't seen her for more than eight years. I didn't want to ring Nana to find out because she wasn't in great health and I didn't want to worry her. Fortunately, Kayla knew how to use social media to find Mum, and we sent her a message on Facebook. Mum replied and we arranged to meet. That was a good start. Mum was living in a townhouse with a housemate.

Journal entry

Saturday, 27 September 2014

I messaged my mum today and said we would be up on the Gold Coast next week for a few days and I wanted to catch up with her. She said 'yes' and seemed good so I don't know how to feel. It will obviously be good – I haven't seen her in eight years. I'm sure when it gets closer, I'll be nervous. Just have to remember: STRONG, CONFIDENT, FEARLESS!!

Journal entry

Wednesday, 1 October 2014

I saw my mum yesterday for the first time in eight years! I was really nervous on my way there but, once I got there, it wasn't bad at all. She was with her housemate so we couldn't talk about things too much. But we just spoke about what's been happening and some small talk. I guess over the next few times I'll be able to open up more and talk about things properly. It's actually really sad because for so long I've had so much hurt and hate towards her but I can't believe this is her life now. She has no job, not many people in her life and I'm assuming she has been like this for a long time. And, when she needed me and Nana the most, we couldn't help her. For all I know, that could have contributed to her health. But I can't look back too much now. We need to talk about things to clear the air and then move forward. Life is too short. Family is the only thing that matters.

A few days later, Kayla and I took Mum out for breakfast. It was the first time that Kayla had met Mum and they hit it off well. Conversation didn't come naturally between Mum and me but Kayla was the spark that got the words flowing. It was a great way to finish my first meetings with Mum in such a long time. There was sadness over those days – we shed some tears together – but there was also brightness, from knowing that we had reunited. The photos that we took of those meetings show Mum and I with smiles on our faces, which was the best sign that we were both glad to see each other. While I was on the Gold Coast, I was able to see Nana for the first time in a few months. Her health was deteriorating as she struggled with dementia. I needed to draw on the resilience skills I had learnt because it was difficult to see Nana like this, particularly as I so fondly remembered her capably caring for me over many years. But at least Nana had excellent care and I knew that I would be able to see her more often in the coming months.

I was still unsure where I would play the following season. The Knights had agreed to let me leave my contract one year early. They were organising to pay the money still outstanding from the two previous years. I didn't want people to feel sorry for me, because I was fine. Players put their bodies on the line in every game and risk the criticism of the footy world when they make mistakes. If players can't accept that, they should look for another career. I received plenty of criticism for my stint at the Knights and some of it was warranted. Fans expected a lot from me and I wanted to deliver for them.

I returned to Newcastle, packed up the house and prepared it for sale. That helped me come to terms with my departure from a city that had seen me at my worst. The old version of me would have fled Newcastle, never wanting to think of my time there. But the new version of me knew that I had to confront the situations that I had created. I was grateful for the opportunity and the experience that Newcastle provided me. I had to get to rock bottom before I could start the journey back up. If I didn't hit rock bottom in Newcastle, it would have happened somewhere else. It may have happened after I retired, and that wouldn't have been good.

Sydney became my temporary home as Kayla found an apartment that she loved. I was happy for her because she had good friends there and she deserved to be happy. Kayla wanted me to decide where I would play in 2015 but she couldn't guarantee that she would go with me. There was interest from some clubs but the Broncos had always been my favourites. I was at a stage in life when I wanted to go home and start again with the club that I had grown up supporting. I knew that I was closer to the end of my career than the start, so this contract was important to me. And I wanted to follow up on one of the recommendations from my stay at the clinic – to begin working in the mental health space. I knew that Brisbane would be a good base to start that work.

My return to the Broncos was announced on 21 November 2014. It was a three-year deal. I left Kayla in Sydney and returned to live on the Gold Coast, finding a temporary home with Kayla's mum, Pepa, her husband, Neil, and their son Chad, who was twelve years younger than me. I was grateful that they took me in because signing with the Broncos had happened quickly and I had to return home in a hurry. Pepa and Neil had a spare room that was perfect for me, but I went there knowing that there was no guarantee that Kayla would follow me back to south-east Queensland.

I fondly remember my first day back at the Broncos – I drove up from the Gold Coast and became emotional as I got close to the club, driving along the streets that I had been down so many times in the first years of my NRL career. I was back at a club that I never wanted to leave in the first place – but I was so glad that I had left. I was a much better person for leaving and returning. If I had never left the Broncos, I suspect that I wouldn't have confronted my problems until it was too late.

Journal entry
Monday, 24 November 2014

My first day back at the Broncos. I was really nervous on the drive. But once I got there it really was like I had never left. Everyone was really welcoming. Such a great club.

I'm so happy and lucky to be back. I met most players and staff and then I had a press conference which went really well. I miss Kayla but I know that this will make us stronger. I'm so grateful for what I've learnt lately and all the things I have in my life. I'm very lucky and now it's up to me to show that and give back. Exciting times ahead. I can't wait to look back and read through here in six or twelve months time! Who knows what will be . . . could be anything . . . STRONG. CONFIDENT. FEARLESS.

Well, for the only time in my life I was a prophet. 'Anything' would happen in those next twelve months.

GRATITUDE
2015–

CHAPTER 13

A girl and a grand final

STATISTICS HAVE NEVER BEEN AT THE FRONT OF MY MIND during my rugby league career, but a few numbers were going through my head after a pre-season training session on Friday, 5 December 2014. How many training sessions and footy games had I racked up in my nine years as a professional footy player? It would have been at least a thousand. That's how long I had gone before I suffered the first serious injury of my career. During the session in the Brisbane summer heat, I ruptured my Achilles tendon.

Journal entry
Saturday, 6 December 2014
Not the best news – I tore my Achilles at training yesterday!!
I'm getting surgery on Tuesday but it looks like I'll be out for

at least six months. I don't think I could have done anything to prevent it. I was doing shuttle runs for fitness and it was getting a little sore but then it just popped. I knew what I'd done straight away. Now I've got to be strong and push through it. The positive is that it will give me more time to work on myself and to do the charity/community work that I need to do. It might even make me release more and let go of footy a bit, so that when I eventually retire, it's not as hard. I'm sure that getting through this, on top of the last few months, will only make me stronger. It's funny how things happen sometimes. There's not much I can do about it apart from moving forward. I have been really loving life. But I'll get back there. This is the time when I need to be the strongest. Don't give in. Only I can do this!

As I got my mind around the injury, my thoughts went to the 2015 State of Origin series. I had not missed a game for the Maroons since I made my debut in 2008, so that became my benchmark for recovery. I wanted to get back in time to play for the Broncos and to prove that I was ready to play the opening Origin match on Wednesday, 27 May 2015. That would be less than six months after my injury. It would be tough, given that I had been told six months was a minimum timeframe for my rehabilitation, let alone returning earlier to prove that I was fit enough for Origin. I researched on the internet other athletes who had torn their Achilles and I found a Baltimore Ravens player in the American National Football League who had returned in five months. That was the hope I needed.

Away from the field, my Achilles injury was about to become a flashpoint for my marriage to Kayla. We were maintaining our relationship long-distance, with Kayla happily going about her life in Sydney, trying to recharge her career and turning her attention to her health. I understood that the previous few months had been tough on Kayla as well as me. I had been to the clinic and had my rehabilitation plan but I felt that Kayla also needed her own time to deal with the last few months. When I rang to tell her that I was injured and facing months of recovery, her reaction was not as caring as I'd hoped. Kayla promised to come up to the Gold Coast to see me but, on the day she was supposed to arrive, she didn't appear. Kayla had decided not to visit and she hadn't let me know. I didn't take that well and struggled to understand why. We had a huge argument over the phone about our marriage. Kayla insisted she was tired of always having to rush to my side when I wasn't doing well. She accused me of playing the victim and told me that my reaction gave her flashbacks to my behaviour prior to my time in the clinic.

Our argument was a reminder that the issues in our marriage were a long way from being repaired. I had a bunch of 'open doors' to close and this one was taking longer to settle than I had hoped. But I should have known that three weeks in the clinic wouldn't cure all of my struggles – there was a lot of work ahead. Kayla came to visit me on the Gold Coast for Christmas and New Year, with the intention of returning to Sydney after a few weeks. In her mind, her trip to the Gold Coast was a 'make-or-break' test for our marriage.

If we didn't work out a way to move forward during those few weeks, Kayla was likely to move on. Either way, she intended to go back to Sydney in early January, which meant that our long-distance marriage would continue for a while longer. Fortunately, I was able to improve my mood when Kayla arrived and we had the best Christmas I'd experienced since I was a child. We had Christmas lunch at Kayla's family's house, joined by Nana and my mum. It was a day built around family, which made it special for me. The year of 2014 was finishing in a much better way than it had appeared five months earlier. Kayla and I then went to Byron Bay with friends over the New Year. We had a great time, with Kayla telling me that this was how a marriage should be – spending quality time together, sharing emotions and enjoying being with our good friends. But the return to training gave me a jolt.

Journal entry

Monday, 5 January 2015

I've been struggling the last few days. I had my first day back at training today which was good but I think it really hit me how hard this is going to be. A lot harder than I thought. I need to get into a good routine and try to get back to being proactive and busy. I need to go over my rehab notes from the clinic more and write in here more. It instantly makes me feel better. I really need to remember how far I have come. Reading back, I've done a lot, and sure, I fell back into some things like sulking,

being sad, angry, negative, but that's when I need to look
at the bigger picture: my goals, my belief, my standards.
I know I can be so, so happy and that's the person I
want to be. That's the person that Kayla deserves to see.
EVERYTHING HAPPENS FOR A REASON. I CAN AND
WILL BENEFIT FROM THIS.

Kayla and I had been getting on well, but we were taking
small steps. Things were promising enough for Kayla to
decide to stay on in the Gold Coast, so we moved into a rental
house, although she still had a lease on her Sydney unit. Kayla
had begun to focus heavily on her health – starting with a
strict fitness routine – because the emotional challenges of the
previous six months had taken a toll. But, in early February,
she began to feel unwell, complaining of tiredness and a
lack of energy. Those feelings increased over a few weeks
and sparked another argument between us. Kayla became
completely frustrated; she felt that every time she came to
my side, her own health deteriorated. She had given me so
much over recent years, and she believed that her health was
struggling as a result. Kayla finally went to see a doctor to get
to the bottom of why she was feeling so unwell. The doctor
sent her for a blood test.

Journal entry
Thursday, 19 February 2015
Kayla has been up and down for a few weeks. She got
tests today to see if there was a problem. She is actually

> pregnant!! I was a little shocked, started to smile, had a
> weird feeling then got a little upset – happy tears.

I had written a few months earlier that anything could happen in the next twelve months, and look what occurred: I blew my Achilles, Kayla moved back to the Gold Coast, my mum returned to my life and then Kayla became pregnant. All within three months. But pregnancy wasn't something we had planned or even discussed, so the news rocked us. It was a complete shock. Kayla's mind immediately went back to her youth. She was born to a seventeen-year-old mother and a twenty-year-old father. They separated three years later. Understandably, Kayla wanted to bring her first child into a marriage that was solid and sustainable. Our marriage was neither of those things, so the idea of the pregnancy scared Kayla. We broke the news to her mum and stepfather who were genuinely excited. We were clearly not as excited, but that wasn't because we didn't want the baby – the news had quite simply blindsided us. Kayla's mum gave her some encouragement – if we had stuck together after all that had been thrown at us in recent years, then we would handle a baby. And Pepa reminded us that we would both be twenty-eight years old when this baby was born, which was a lot later in life than when she had Kayla.

The news gave me a chance to reflect on how I was coping with my recovery. And I found that I was handling things better than I had expected. I was opening up more to people close to me, including Jan Earl, George Mimis and Wayne

Bennett, and I was having better and deeper conversations than I had ever had. Having Mum back in my life, visiting regularly, had eased my stress. I felt loved and cared for in a way that I could not recall feeling before. My mindset had changed. I knew that I was better prepared to support Kayla and become a father than I had ever been.

Looking back now, the Achilles injury was the best thing that could have happened to me. Kayla has often said that. I had only been out of the clinic for four months and I still had some progress to make. The injury meant that it would be at least ten months between matches. That was a good opportunity for me to continue to develop my mental health, concentrate on our marriage and to begin some ambassadorial work.

At about the same time, I was approached by ABC Television's *Australian Story* program to be the subject of an upcoming episode. *Australian Story* is a thirty-minute weekly show that looks at one person, interviewing them and their friends and family to tell the story of their life. I thought about it for a while and realised it would be a huge opportunity to tell people my story. Even though I was entering my tenth year in the NRL, details of my life were little known, with the exception of my visit to a mental health clinic. I had never sought publicity, I didn't use social media and I didn't speak publicly about myself often. From the outside, my life was mysterious and I knew that enabled people to fill in the gaps for themselves. *Australian Story* took some time to film. There were several interviews with me, a separate interview with Kayla and an interview with Wayne spliced together with some insights from journalists who covered rugby league. There was also an interview with Nana and Mum, who I felt did well to tell their stories about me. The program was emotional to watch when it aired. It was a strange feeling to sit and take in a half-hour show about my life that touched on some tender moments. But I was glad that I did it. The show was another positive step in my aim to raise awareness about mental health challenges.

Journal entry

Sunday, 8 March 2015

The footy season is back. The boys had the first game on Thursday, Round 1, versus the Rabbitohs. I went and watched and helped out where I could. It wasn't too bad watching. We got pumped, which wasn't good but it's early days so nothing to worry about yet. Kayla and I went to Newcastle for the weekend and stayed at Macca and Teigan's place, which was good. I felt quite weird and uncomfortable when we got to Newcastle, bringing back old memories, which I didn't like. But once we got to their house it was a lot better. It was really good to see them. When I get into those situations in which I don't feel good, I have to remember to be strong, confident, fearless. I need to remember how lucky I am to be where I am now. LIFE'S GOOD.

The NRL season didn't begin well for the Broncos, falling 36–6 to the defending premiers South Sydney. The critics didn't know what to make of the Broncos in 2015. We had Wayne back and we had a strong mix of older and younger players. I reunited with a few of our older players – Justin Hodges was captain while Corey Parker and Sam Thaiday were the leaders of the forward pack. The backline was different from the last one I had played in with Brisbane. Ben Hunt and Anthony Milford, two of the emerging stars of the NRL, were in our halves with the ability to turn a game in a second with their speed and quick footwork. Corey Oates was on the wing in his third NRL season. It was difficult to predict how our season would play out but we knew we had the talent to beat any team.

After the opening loss, the Broncos clicked into gear with a five-game winning streak that made the league take notice. That included a Round 3 thrashing of the Cowboys, who were winless and being written off by the media for the season. The criticism of the Cowboys was only dangerous, though, if they took notice of it. The flow of the footy season does not match the media cycle. After every match, a team can find fault in their performance. That's because footy players are human and make mistakes. The key is to know which mistakes need attention. Good players, good coaches and good teams know when they have serious problems that need fixing. If the Broncos had believed the media reports about our five-game losing streak after the Origin series in 2006, we would have packed up early and started our end-of-season trip. Wayne was continually asked during that losing streak if we were in a 'slump'. He denied it every time. 'Your definition of a slump and mine are different,' Wayne kept telling reporters. When we won the premiership that season, it was clear that Wayne was right. In 2010, the Dragons copped it from the media before we won the grand final. We were criticised all year for not having enough attacking ability. But we defended so well that we won the grand final. The St George Illawarra team of early 2011 was probably the best team that I played in throughout my club career – but we didn't win a finals match that year.

One of the reasons that I tried to avoid reading stories about myself for most of my career is that the media tended to overreact to each weekend's results. A big win early in the season is likely to start speculation of the winner's premiership hopes. Three losses in a row is apparently a time for panic. That's not a criticism of journalists – they're doing their job and they clearly believe that audiences are more interested in stories about losing teams than winning teams. One game for each club represents about 4 per cent of the season. It's wise not to overreact to one game. Every team will suffer good and bad patches throughout any season. The salary cap usually makes sure of that. And the competition is played over twenty-six rounds so that the most consistent teams are rewarded with the best draws for the finals. After that, it comes down to the best team on the day and how each team handles the pressure of the big moments. That's why a rugby league season is so fair.

The Broncos didn't seem to have too many problems early in 2015 as we surged to the top of the table. That was great news for me as I prepared to return from my Achilles injury. I was well ahead of schedule in my rehabilitation and I was now thinking that I could play again within five months of the injury. That had been my goal all along and I had taken no chances with my recovery, doing every piece of rehabilitation possible, including a lot of pool work. My biggest concern was my weight – I was too heavy – which had rarely been a problem for me. I changed my diet to make sure that I could lose the weight before playing again. I returned to full training in the second week of April with a view to playing against the Panthers at Suncorp Stadium in Round 9. That would give me enough time to play two matches before the State of Origin team was picked.

When match day against the Panthers came around on 8 May, I was more worried about my right hamstring than my Achilles. But I was ready to go against a Penrith team that came to Suncorp Stadium with a 4–4 win–loss record. This was my first game of rugby league since 20 July 2014 – a break of almost ten months. So much had happened since that last game. I returned to football a completely different person with a different outlook. I did a series of media interviews while I was injured, talking openly about my progress since leaving the clinic. I was confident that, whatever happened in this Friday night game, I wouldn't spend the rest of the weekend hiding away at home. My journal had no entries from 25 April until 15 June – a sign that I was coping well with life. However, my return to footy was still kept relatively quiet – Wayne wanted to keep something up his sleeve. So, only a few hours before the game, I was confirmed for my return at fullback, wearing the unusual No. 18 jersey because I hadn't been named in the original team.

This was a game unlike any I had played in. With one minute to go, we were staring at a loss to a Panthers team that had not scored a try. Two penalty goals and a Matt Moylan field goal in the seventy-fifth minute had pushed Penrith to a 5–4 lead. Ben Hunt's field goal attempt in the seventy-seventh minute floated to the right of the posts, leaving us desperate for a final crack at victory. And that's when Benny showed the skills that would become so important to our club. With one minute remaining, Benny decided against settling for another field goal. He called the ball to the right edge and slipped a short pass for a charging Corey Oates to crash over for a try. We won 8–5.

Benny and Anthony Milford were unstoppable when they were in form. They were very different halves from the likes of Cooper Cronk, who loved planning and structure. Benny and Milf preferred to play what was in front of them. If they could spot an opportunity against a defensive line, they were usually quick enough to take it. If the forwards were providing space, Benny and Milf were happy to back themselves to make the most of their opportunities. They were exciting to play with when they were in that form. Sometimes, I had no idea what they were going to do so it was hard for defences to prepare to stop them.

The Broncos' winning run came to an end in Round 10 against a Cowboys team that had recovered from its opening three losses to pile on seven straight wins. That night, they completed all thirty-four attacking sets, earning praise in the media for 'perfection'. That certainly was a long way from the death notices written by journalists after Round 3. I got through both matches unscathed and was selected for the Origin series opener. That was a big moment for me. That selection was my goal from the moment I snapped my Achilles, and I had made it.

Origin camp that year was a new experience for almost every Queensland player – we were going into the series without holding the Origin shield. This made Mal Meninga's task of motivating us much easier than usual – not that I can recall Mal ever having any trouble with that. But once again, Mal was handed a massive free kick when the Sydney media started criticising us for being too old. Yes, the Queensland squad that had lost the 2014 series was back together, but that didn't mean the selectors had made a mistake. We were still the best squad for the job at hand. The Sydney media were upbeat because the Blues were the reigning champions and Game I was at the Olympic Stadium. But the man we missed the most in 2014 – halfback Cooper Cronk – returned and became the star. Coops scored early but we fell behind as the Blues scored two consecutive tries. We levelled the score with twenty-five minutes to go before a classic Origin finish. The deadlock was broken in the seventy-fourth minute when Coops seemed to have all the time in the world to kick a field goal that put us ahead 11–10. He was so calm that he looked like he was at training. That was the final scoring play in a result that showed we weren't too old and that Mal was still the best Origin coach in the business.

We lost Game II in Melbourne as Greg Inglis's length-of-the-field try was disallowed before the Blues scored twice late to set up a decider. We had the finale that we wanted – a showdown at Suncorp Stadium to make it nine series in ten years. Cameron Smith would equal Darren Lockyer's record of thirty-six Origin matches for Queensland, while Justin Hodges would play his final Maroons match. Queensland teams never needed extra motivation but we had been so close as a squad for the last decade that players' milestones meant something for the whole team. We didn't want them to end with a loss.

News about the decider was overtaken, however, by Alex McKinnon's appearance on a national current affairs TV show a few days before the game. Macca spoke in depth about his injury and his rehabilitation. In one part of the story, Macca became upset when he watched footage of the game in which he was injured. The story focused on Cameron Smith arguing against a penalty for the players who had tackled Macca, claiming that Macca was to blame because of the way he ducked his head when being tackled. Macca struggled with Smithy's words to the referee – while his attitude towards his injury and his rehabilitation had been incredible, Macca was still emotional about the events of that night. That was totally understandable.

Some media outlets portrayed Smithy as a bad guy. The perception was that he was heartless. It was an easy story for the media to publish. But it wasn't true. I had known him for the best part of a decade and Smithy was a first-class person. I had played almost fifty games with him and plenty of games against him. It's not in Smithy's nature to go out and hurt people. He's not a sledger and he's not a villain. He's simply one of the most competitive blokes I've ever played with or against. Smithy wants to win everything – footy, golf, computer games or whatever else comes up. If you were in a room together, he'd race you to the door. That's Smithy.

Because he's competitive, Smithy will look for any advantage possible, including trying to talk the referee out of a penalty after Macca was tackled. But Smithy had no idea how badly Macca was hurt. No one knew just how serious it would become. Smithy was as shocked as anyone when word spread about the severity of Macca's injury. Smithy is usually a very calm guy with an easygoing attitude to games. I've been near him during stoppages in play and you're likely to get a smile and a joke from him even when you're on opposite teams. But I've never seen Smithy get angry or throw punches. That's not his style.

Smithy is one of the best rugby league players the game has seen. He's the man with the body that we all liked to laugh about – there's no abdominal sixpack and no muscle definition. But get one-on-one with Smithy in a wrestling drill at training and you quickly understand his strength. He'll squeeze the life out of you. He was always one of the best performers in the gym. When he plays, he's just as much a coach on the field as a player. And when the coach is touching the ball in almost every attacking play and he's surrounded by quality players, you know his team will be hard to beat. People often talk about the need to have a good halfback to win premierships. When you have a great player like Smithy who is so involved on the field, he becomes much more valuable than a halfback. He's been so integral to the success of every team that he's played in that Smithy should always be regarded as a great of the game.

He was also the best motivator among any of my teammates. Wayne and Mal could reel off inspiring speeches that fired up players for big occasions. They spoke with passion, they spoke with emotion and they knew how to deliver a punchline. Smithy wasn't far behind them. He could work a dressing room at half-time in a close game. He could unleash some stirring words behind the posts. He was professional in everything he did. When you have a physical build like Smithy's that isn't exactly bursting with muscles, you know that you can't beat too many guys with crunching tackles. You have to beat them with heart, and no one could ever question Smithy's courage and determination.

The negative media coverage helped focus Smithy like never before as he prepared for the Origin decider, although he didn't let his emotions affect the squad. Will Chambers moved into the centres that night as Greg Inglis went to fullback to replace the injured Billy Slater. We expected that it would be another close game but this was a blowout – an Origin record 52–6 win over the Blues to claim the series.

This was the most dominant display of any Origin game I played in. We were simply superb and the Blues were out on their feet.

The home crowd was as loud as I had ever heard it. As I learnt, the only thing louder than a Queensland crowd cheering for the Maroons in a close game is a crowd cheering for us to extend our lead to almost 50 points. They were deafening and they never let up on the Blues. It would turn out to be Mal's last game as Queensland coach. He had established the most dominant coaching record in Origin's history and created a legacy for a new generation. He had ensured that the hunger that drove that Queensland team through the 1980s was still driving the same team thirty years later. It had been a pleasure to play for him.

The Origin success rolled into more wins at the Broncos, where we avoided an immediate post-Origin slump. We won our first three games after the Origin decider by a combined scoreline of 92–24, remaining in first place on the NRL ladder. This time the previous year, I was heading for my stint at the mental health clinic. That followed the Knights' terrible loss to the Gold Coast Titans in the Rise For Alex round. Twelve months on, the Broncos defeated the Titans 34–0 at Suncorp Stadium. The difference in the scorelines from those matches twelve months apart reflected the changes in my personal life. I kept my mind focused on the tips that I learnt at the mental health clinic and they were helping me immensely. Kayla and I were now only two months away from the birth of our first child. We learnt that we would have a girl.

Journal entry

Monday, 27 July 2015

So much has happened since I last wrote in here but I probably won't remember it all. Broncos are going great. We have won eight in a row and we're on top of the ladder. My form has been getting better each week which gives me a lot of confidence. It's only ten weeks to go now until our little girl arrives. That time will fly. It's very exciting. I've still been seeing my therapist which has been good.

My therapist had become an important part of my rehabilitation. I couldn't walk out of the clinic and expect to have my problems solved – I was told that I needed help along the way. Jan Earl had become a constant support for me since she helped me at the clinic and had recommended a good therapist in Brisbane. I would see him about once a month and each time I saw him I was reminded of how necessary the visits were for me. I could talk about how my life was going and how I could continue to close the 'open doors' that I had identified at the clinic. I had to look at it as a journey of continual practice to make sure I was the best person I could be.

Kayla and I were enjoying our marriage as the birth of our little girl edged closer. We were both excited and Kayla seemed to be handling all of the preparations with ease. Kayla said that the pregnancy had provided her with a calmness and focus. Kayla had never wanted to be a 'WAG' – one of the so-called wives and girlfriends of professional athletes. It is often used as a derogatory term and it didn't fit most of the wives and girlfriends I knew, and especially someone with Kayla's drive and creativity. She was unable to focus on her career as the pregnancy reached the last trimester but she found a purpose in preparing to be a mum. Pepa's words to her daughter had been correct – Kayla had overcome so much in her life that she would handle the challenge of motherhood. And the pregnancy had drawn us closer together. Our relationship was back to how a marriage should feel.

Despite the positives in my life occurring both on and off the field, over the final weeks of the regular season I was finding football tough as we traded wins and losses. We lost first place when we fell to the Roosters in an epic Round 24 match, but we were good enough to finish the regular season in second place, putting us in line for a home clash with the Cowboys in week one of the finals, with a weekend off awaiting the winner. I felt like I needed that quick break more than ever before. I had copped a series of knocks in recent weeks that left me feeling sore for days. Then I received news that forced me to draw on all of my skills learnt at the mental health clinic. Our routine before the finals match against the Cowboys would be different from a normal home game – we would spend the night in a hotel in Brisbane to prepare. That decision was made two days before the game, when I had already started to focus on my preparation. My adjustment disorder, as diagnosed at the clinic, identified the difficulties I had in responding well to sudden change.

Journal entry

Friday, 11 September 2015

I just feel off. One of the reasons is definitely FOOTY!! My performances of late have been down and the team has been down. I suppose the pressure of finals is larger than we thought. I feel like my motivation levels are low and it's harder to get up for a game. I hurt my back three weeks ago. It's heaps better but I'm still feeling it. Now I'm having to stay at a hotel tonight in Brisbane, which makes preparation for our game different. That really pissed me off. I would much rather do my own thing than have to stay at hotels and stick to the usual away schedule. And only getting sent the memo the day before was another thing that annoyed me. I know when I get there and get to the game I'll be fine. But I'm just not liking the feelings I'm getting now. Maybe I'm just having a bad day. I've got to remember how far I have come. I would have loved to be here one year ago. SMILE. FUN!!

That was an unusual entry in my journal, but I couldn't expect to walk away from the clinic and face no challenges. The difference was that I could write a journal entry like that and overcome it quickly because I had learnt ways to cope. Before I went to the clinic, that feeling could go on for days or even weeks. Accompanying that emotion was my uncertainty about the Broncos' finals chances, as I felt our intensity at training had dropped. As I got older, I realised that I was running out of chances to play in another premiership team. I thought that this Broncos team could win a grand final but the drop in our intensity had me worried. I spoke to Wayne about my concerns as we prepared to face the Cowboys. We knew this would be a tough game – the Cowboys had beaten us in Round 10 in Townsville and they had Johnathan Thurston. The game was as close as we expected and we were forced to rely heavily on our defence. We scored two tries thanks to our smaller men. Benny Hunt scored a great solo try in the first half, while Kodi Nikorima, playing in his first finals match, split the Cowboys through the middle in the second half before finding Anthony Milford to run away for a try. That placed us ahead 16–6 with fifteen minutes remaining, but we knew the Cowboys would come at us again. They did, in the seventieth minute when J.T. pounced on a short kick near the line to bring the scores back to 16–12. Those last ten minutes were tough but we were good enough to win, gaining a weekend off.

I had never been so glad to have a break in a finals series. And to defend so well convinced me that we weren't fading as the season progressed. That meant that I could prepare for the birth of our daughter before our preliminary final at Suncorp Stadium. The timing was superb – instead of arriving on her due date on the day after the grand final, our little girl was born three days before the preliminary final on Tuesday, 22 September at 6 p.m. We named her Willow Kamila Boyd and our lives were changed from that moment.

I was filled with pride when I held Willow for the first time. I was emotional from a combination of joy at starting our own family and also pride in Kayla. She was awesome throughout her pregnancy and seemed such a natural mum. I stayed with Kayla and Willow at the hospital as Kayla and I both adjusted to this new person in our lives. The shock of the news in February had been replaced by a feeling of contentment and relaxation. I had learnt the hard way that football wasn't the most important thing in life and now we had a family to raise together.

I have been asked how someone with adjustment disorder coped with the arrival of a baby. That wasn't a problem for me – I'd had most of the year to prepare, so I was as ready as I would ever be when Kayla gave birth. But the second night of Willow's life was an early reminder of our new situation. Willow was unsettled and cried for much of the night. Kayla and I didn't sleep, but I had an important match coming up in a few days so Kayla told me to go home and get some rest.

The weekend off was a boon for the Broncos, giving us every chance to qualify for the grand final by beating the Roosters at home. There was an air of excitement in Brisbane for the Friday night game – almost 52 000 were in the stands – and I was still on a high from Willow's birth. The game started in a way that none of us could have expected. We received the ball and went through our first attacking set, getting to a clearing kick within the opening fifty seconds. The kick went to Roosters winger Shaun Kenny-Dowall, who picked the ball up within a metre of the sideline. I was chasing the kick. My thought process had always been to run myself ragged early to get into games, including running hard on kick-chases.

We had spoken before the game about the Roosters' desire to get the ball to fullback Roger Tuivasa-Sheck in the middle as often as they could. With that in mind, I ran a line between Shaun and Roger to prevent a pass. At no stage did I expect Shaun to actually pass the ball. When I started to think he might actually pass, I sprinted and arrived just in time for a floating pass directed at Roger to hit me in the chest before a twenty-metre run to an open tryline. Inside one minute, we led the preliminary final 6–0.

We scored three tries within the opening eighteen minutes and, despite a Roosters fightback, we were able to finish them off for a 31–12 win. The Cowboys had also qualified for the grand final, placing us in an all-Queensland decider that captured the attention of a state. Just the prospect of two Queensland teams in the grand final was exciting. It would be the fourth time that we had played the Cowboys in 2015. We arrived in Sydney a few days before the game and saw plenty of Cowboys supporters around. They wished us good luck and we wished them the same – it was that type of atmosphere.

More than twelve months earlier, I had written in my journal about the importance of gratitude. Heading into October 2015, I had a lot for which I could be grateful. Willow was doing well in her early days and Kayla was a brilliant mum. I had the chance to introduce Willow to my mum and Nana, adding another generation to our small family. Football was going well and I was fortunate to be playing in my third grand final in my tenth season in the NRL. I knew some players went through long careers without reaching a grand final, let alone winning a premiership, and I didn't take that for granted, particularly as I headed closer to the end of my career.

The grand final was always going to be tough. Our teams knew each other well and we knew how evenly matched we were, so it was impossible to be confident of the result. We started well with a long-range try to Corey Oates in the eighth minute, before the Cowboys scored twice to take the lead. We regained the upper hand when Matt Gillett scooped up a lost ball from J.T. before passing to Jack Reed for a try. It's still difficult to think about the last minute of regular time. We were leading 16–12 and had the Cowboys beaten, but they kept the ball alive, passing across the field until they scored in the right corner as the siren went. It was a remarkable try. J.T. then had a conversion to win the match, but it hit the right upright and bounced away. It was time for a sudden-death finish to the season. We started extra time with Benny Hunt dropping the ball from the kick-off. Soon after, J.T. kicked a field goal and the Cowboys won 17–16.

For some of the Cowboys, that would be the most memorable moment of their careers. For some of us in the Broncos, it would be our worst. It was devastating. There is no pretending that game didn't hurt. Losing a grand final in that way is not something you get over easily. In fact, as the years go on, there is still hurt about how close we came. I have always defended Benny, despite the focus that fell on him for the mistake. The simple fact is that we wouldn't have made the grand final that season without him. Benny had a superb year. His combination with Milf had been brilliant. They were key reasons why we had progressed into the last game of the season. Wayne taught me over the years that games aren't won or lost on one play. They're won or lost for a whole bunch of reasons across a game. In the last few minutes of that game, there were a few moments that helped the Cowboys to get to the tryline to tie up the game. Benny had nothing to do with those. We all shared responsibility as a team.

When you lose like that you can forget how good a season we had. The Broncos had a great year in 2015. And I had personally enjoyed a season that I would not have thought possible when I checked into the mental health clinic only fourteen months earlier. I now had eight weeks during the off-season to spend at home with Kayla and Willow. I had been looking forward to this break for a long time. The grand final pain was raw but my family life was as good as I could have hoped. I enjoyed spending time with Kayla and Willow, learning things about each other as we adapted to this new life.

Although I recognised this, there were still challenges for me. I could not expect that two major events in my life – the birth of Willow and the nature of that grand final loss – would not impact someone who struggled with adjustment. Kayla worried that I had not properly dealt with the distress of losing the grand final. She knew that a loss like that only a year or so earlier would have plunged me into a dark period. I was a lot better after this grand final, although Kayla was right to be concerned. At the same time, I had to adjust to the changed dynamic in our marriage. I had become accustomed to receiving Kayla's full attention and using that as my source of strength when I was feeling challenged. But Willow needed Kayla's attention far more than me. I knew that was only natural and I would never have wanted Kayla to prioritise me ahead of Willow. But I still had to adjust to that, and the journey wasn't easy despite the tools that I had learnt at the clinic. It made the small problems in life seem far greater than they were as my mood turned towards anger at times. One of the first entries in my journal instructed me not to overreact to the things that were unimportant. My failure to do that in the lead-up to Christmas was the main reason that I took to my journal for the last time to draft perhaps my most desperate entry. I noted in that entry on 23 December:

Been really struggling the last few days. I don't want to be angry and unhappy around Xmas time. It's just been really hard to snap out of it. I have been thinking really bad thoughts lately. Just been feeling really worthless. I don't think I would ever try to take my life. But when you feel so low sometimes it actually sounds like a good idea. Sometimes I feel like I'm fine and nothing is wrong. But then when I get like this, I realise I'm lying to myself. I just can't handle any little negative things. I let things get to me too easily. I need to remember what is important. And it's not little things or things that go wrong.

I have so much to be grateful for!!

I was right about that – the previous twelve months had given me more than I could have imagined. The upside from my time at the mental health clinic was that I could overcome my dark days much more quickly. By Christmas Day, I was feeling better. I promised myself that I wouldn't spoil our first Christmas as parents by giving in to feelings that I knew I could overcome with the right focus. Christmas 2015 was one I'll always remember – our little gift Willow will not recall it but she was the greatest present that Kayla and I could ever have imagined.

CHAPTER 14

Talking about mental health

One of the reasons that I didn't write in my journal again was that my therapy began to come through my work as a mental health ambassador. After my experience at the clinic, one of my goals for 2016 was to begin my work in this field. With the support I had received, I identified that as an important part of my rehabilitation and I was feeling strong enough to tell my story publicly. Jan Earl continually urged me to speak out because there were few athletes talking openly about their mental health challenges. There was a school of thought within rugby league that players who said they were suffering from poor mental health were only making excuses – these players couldn't handle the pressure so they blamed mental health. I had heard that said about me after I stepped away from footy in 2014. But that was never the case and I doubt that it was true of anyone who admitted that they were struggling. The people making those accusations probably didn't understand mental health. Unfortunately, events in 2015 brought that message home for the rugby league community. Three young NRL-contracted players took their own lives within three months. Their deaths were reported in the media, shining a light on the need to pay closer attention to how young male athletes were coping with the pressures of their lives. I was rattled to hear of those deaths. They were young men who clearly had much to live for but who found themselves in situations they thought were hopeless. I felt for them and I felt for their families and friends. These were devastating losses.

I wanted to continue telling my story to let others know that there was help available. I still had a long way to go in my journey but I was keen to pass on what I had already learnt. I recognised immediately that there was one problem with this plan – I wasn't very good at public speaking. The thought of standing in front of a roomful of complete strangers to share my story was scary. So I sought help to develop my skills. It was hard work at first – I had to learn everything, from voice projection to correct breathing and even what to do with my hands – but I slowly gained the confidence to help me speak to audiences filled with strangers. That would have been unthinkable for me twelve months earlier, but just the fact that I considered doing that was another sign of my progress.

My first steps into this arena were as gentle as possible – I accompanied five other Broncos players and staff to speak at junior footy clubs and schools. These were enthusiastic young audiences who seemed rapt to be able to hear a bunch of Broncos players such as Jack Reed and Jharal Yow Yeh talking about their careers. We did this work for the Broncos and also for an NRL program that promoted positive mental health, which was an important way to reach younger players.

The reactions of the young people we spoke with were always interesting. I could tell when our message hit home and I would see some of them work up the courage to come and speak with us. After giving our presentation at a school one particular day, a girl approached me. We talked for a while, and I recognised in her the signs that I knew too well: she didn't feel good about herself; she didn't have a support network; and she felt that she had no self-worth. I knew that it took a lot of courage for her to discuss those issues with a stranger. We asked her to become involved in some of the wider Broncos schools programs to ensure that we could keep an eye on her progress, and so I saw her a few times after that initial meeting. Those Broncos programs were critical for young women like that. The programs had nothing to do with football – instead they promoted positive thinking and the power of school attendance. We saw that young woman grow in confidence as she learnt skills to cope with her challenges.

The mental health work I carried out was extremely valuable in helping me to reconcile who I was. I knew that I was a good person inside, but the perception that the media portrayed about me played on my mind. My self-confidence needed work, so negative media always affected me. But doing things for others gave me a better idea of who I was, lifting my self-worth.

I wasn't confident enough in early 2016 to accept Wayne's invitation to discuss the Broncos' captaincy. Justin Hodges had just retired, opening the door for the prized position of captain of one of Australia's best-known clubs. Wayne asked me for my thoughts, and I told him that I wasn't ready for it. There were several reasons why. I still had my own struggles and issues to sort out before I could take on a position like that. I didn't think that I had been back at the club long enough – I had only been there for one season and I missed some of that with injury, and I didn't think that I knew the group well enough to lead it. But the major reason was that Corey Parker was playing, and he was the best person for the job. He would do it well and he deserved it, so I was pleased when he was named captain.

The Broncos had plenty to look forward to in 2016. We had almost the same team that had made the grand final in 2015, with the addition of James Roberts in the centres. Jimmy was the fastest player that I had played with or against. He was incredibly quick off the mark, capable of running around his opposing centre or even going wider to run around the winger. That's how fast he was. He was electric. It doesn't matter what sport you're in, speed kills. You can't coach it. And it worries opposing players.

Jimmy drew plenty of interest from the media that year but his early games for the Broncos weren't his best. He broke out in Round 4 during a Good Friday night showdown with the Cowboys at Suncorp Stadium. We had a capacity crowd to watch our first game against the Cowboys since the grand final. It was another tight match. We thought Jimmy and Anthony Milford had clinched the match for us in the seventy-fifth minute when they combined for a 95-metre try that put us two points ahead. We should have known better. Johnathan Thurston kicked a penalty goal in the last minute and we went to extra time again. Fortunately, we won this game when Milf landed a field goal in the eighty-fifth minute. We had an outpouring of celebration, knowing that we had wrestled a game away from the Cowboys.

Despite our win, the Broncos–Cowboys rivalry just wouldn't go away in a season that was jolted by Origin losses. We won seven of our first eight matches but then lost five out of six as the Origin period began. The first of those losses came in Townsville as we fell 19–18 to the Cowboys. This time, we didn't even make it to extra time. J.T. kicked a field goal with five minutes remaining and Ben Hunt's attempt to level the scores in the final minute slid to the right of the posts. Those losses during the Origin period were enough to cost us a top-four berth for the finals – the Origin period was often the difference between a second chance in the finals or a sudden-death match in the first week. We finished fifth on points differential and faced the eighth-placed Titans at home in the opening week. We won to set up another clash with the Cowboys in Townsville in week two of the finals. This would be our seventh match against the Cowboys in two seasons. We lost Jimmy for that match with a suspension, which knocked my confidence simply because his speed could change games. But we had the team to win and it looked that way with ten minutes to go when Corey Oates ran eighty metres to score, putting us ahead 20–18. You can guess what happened after that – J.T. kicked a penalty goal in the final minute to send us to another golden-point period. This time, it wasn't death by field goal. It was death by class as J.T. and Michael Morgan combined for a try that won the game, killed our season and ended Corey Parker's career at 347 games.

It was a tough way for our season to end, especially because we knew we had a team that was good enough to go all the way. But the Cowboys were our nemesis again. And the rivalry didn't end with that season. In Round 2, 2017, they would beat us in extra time yet again. I've been asked repeatedly why we played so many close games during that period. The reason is quite simple: we were two teams that liked to play football. At the time, the game was being affected by wrestling that helped tacklers to slow down the speed of the attacking set. When we played the Cowboys, there wasn't a lot of wrestle. And there weren't many penalties. There was just a lot of football. There were also a lot of players in both teams who knew each other and had played for both clubs so they understood the other team and were motivated to play well. And, of course, the Cowboys had J.T. so they were never out of a game. The best thing about those games was the spirit in which they were played. They were our toughest games of the year but they were played in the spirit befitting two Queensland teams.

The golden-point rule was introduced before I started playing in the NRL, so I've never known any different. I would prefer that games in extra time were decided by the first team to score a try rather than a single point. Just as the Cowboys won our 2016 semifinal, teams should score a try to ensure a fair result. By the time you get to golden point, you're gassed, and the match becomes a race for a field goal rather than a try. The approach is simple: if you take the ball from the kick-off, you probably won't get a chance to get into field-goal range during those six tackles. You will get as far down the field as possible and then bomb into the corner, chase hard and try to defend. Then you hope to get the ball back in a better position to get into field-goal range on the next set. It doesn't make for the best viewing – it's a clinical approach to scoring 1 point.

We almost needed another golden-point period for the first game of the 2016 Origin series, which ended with a scoreless second half. We were fortunate enough to win that match 6–4, giving Kevin Walters an encouraging start to his career as Origin coach. Kevvie had taken over from Mal Meninga, whose ten years in charge of the Maroons included a 20–10 win–loss record and nine winning series. It was a tough act for Kevvie to follow but he did well by not making too many changes to our camp. Kevvie was already a footy legend, with twenty Origin appearances and an incredible six premierships. He had enormous respect from all of the squad, which had some new faces in 2016 with Justin Hodges retired and Billy Slater injured. Kevvie ran his Origin camps in a similar way to Mal and he wasn't dissimilar in the way he motivated the squad. Kevvie wore his heart on his sleeve and his passion for Queensland was easy to see and believe.

Billy's absence meant that I was selected to play fullback for Queensland for the first time. I was pumped to get the role because it was my preferred position and I was playing well there for the Broncos. But I didn't expect the move to make me so nervous. Before the opening match, I was as nervous as I had ever been for a game of footy. When I was playing a club game, I would usually start to get nervous on the day before a game. With Origin, that extended to a few days. I couldn't stop thinking about this match from the moment that we went into camp because I simply didn't want to let anyone down. A good or bad game at fullback can be the difference between winning and losing. That may not always be the case on the wing, where I had played each of my previous twenty-three Origin matches.

The only way that I could deal with nerves was through practice. I did extra work leading into that match, including plenty of work taking high balls. That helped my confidence as we headed to Sydney for the series opener.

In the end, my nerves were unfounded – I played all three matches at fullback and Queensland won the series 2–1. We were two minutes away from a clean sweep until the Blues scored late to win the final match at the Olympic Stadium. I was rapt for our squad and for Kevvie, who overcame the pressure of replacing Mal to almost deliver us to three wins. I received the Ron McAuliffe Medal that year as Queensland's player of the series, which was something I would treasure. It was among the highlights in a year I rate as perhaps my best for individual form. I also received the Broncos' highest honour – the Paul Morgan Medal – for my play across the NRL season. My good form was enabled by my life off the field, which was going as well as I could have hoped. Rugby league was no longer the single focus of my life – it was still very important to me, but my family was my priority and that helped my footy.

I headed to England for the Four Nations tournament to finish the 2016 season comfortable with my spot in the Australian team. It would be the beginning of a new era in the Kangaroos because Mal Meninga had taken over as coach. There was some speculation after another heated Origin series that Mal may struggle to win the support of the Blues players he had plotted against during his illustrious career as Queensland coach. But Mal told journalists it would not be a problem because, in his vast experience, Australian teams always came together. He was right. The squad at the Four Nations played well for Mal and enjoyed the new touches he brought to the Kangaroos. He tried to bring honour and prestige to the jersey, ensuring we understood that we were chosen as the best players in the country. We went into the Four Nations tournament without the world number one ranking and Mal was determined that we would regain it.

We were unbeaten leading into the final against New Zealand at the Anfield stadium in Liverpool. This was our chance to win the tournament and regain the top ranking, but despite this, I wasn't nervous for this game, playing fullback in a backline that included Cooper Cronk, J.T., Blake Ferguson, Greg Inglis, Josh Dugan and Valentine Holmes. In fact, my Test appearances for Australia were the games that I was least likely to be nervous about. I continued to find that playing for Australia meant that you were playing with the best of the best and everyone around you did their job. We knew we could win every game that we played in. We won the final comfortably against the Kiwis, building a 28–0 lead before a final score of 34–8.

I had so much to be grateful for in rugby league in 2016. And I had a lot to give thanks for off the field. The bumps of 2015 had given way to a smoother ride for Kayla and me, as we both enjoyed a year in which our young family grew with the arrival of Willow. I still had my times of struggle but, with the continued help of a therapist and utilising the tools that I learnt at the clinic, I was making sure I could cope with the setbacks that would always be a part of my life.

CHAPTER 15

Time to captain

WHEN WAYNE BENNETT ASKED ME TO BE BRONCOS CAPTAIN in 2017, I was much more willing to consider his invitation than I was twelve months earlier. I thought back to my first-grade debut at the club. I was the eighteen-year-old in the corner of the change room who could barely look his older teammates in the eye. All I wanted was to keep my head down and to not make a mistake in a game. I barely spoke to the older forwards and I would never, ever talk in a team meeting. I was the teenager terrified of being marked down in Wayne's weekly written assessments of players. If I went to a game, played well and didn't say a word to most of the team, I'd had a good day. Now, Wayne was asking me to become the tenth captain of a club that I had supported for as long as I could remember. I felt humbled by the invitation because I had some grasp of the greatness of the nine men who had led the club previously and what they had done for its profile and its standing among supporters.

I accepted Wayne's offer because I felt that I was ready for the responsibility. I never felt completely comfortable in taking on the role because of my shy nature but this was as good as it would get, especially off the back of my form in 2016. I really had no idea what to expect of the role of captain. I had played under many captains during my career and each had a different style. Ben Hornby, Kurt Gidley, Justin Hodges, Corey Parker and Cameron Smith all brought different approaches to their roles. I had admired traits in all of them, although I couldn't model myself on any one of them because I was too different in personality.

There was one player, however, whose leadership style suited me – Darren Lockyer. He was my first NRL captain and he made one of the strongest impressions on me of any player in my career. It wasn't because we talked a lot – in my first three years at the Broncos, the most common words that Locky and I exchanged were 'hi' and 'bye'. But Locky was ultra professional in every part of his game and that was something that I took in. He was always in superb shape but he would never do extra sessions at training – I always suspected he was doing them somewhere else; how could he be so much fitter than those of us who stayed back at training every session? He was incredibly competitive and you knew that he would do whatever he could to win a game for his team.

The main reason that Locky suited me most as a captaincy model was that his leadership was about action rather than words. He had a gravelly voice that didn't lend itself to long, stirring speeches although, when things needed to be said,

Locky said them and the team listened to every word. On the field, he was all about action. He would kick the ball and win the chase. That would spark teammates who would see Locky sprinting down the field. They didn't want to let him down. In my first stint at the Broncos, I remember vividly a perfect two-on-one chance for a try that Locky set up, but instead of staying on my wing I went back underneath him. Locky's pass sailed over the sideline as I ran the other way. He gave me a look that I will never forget. If there was a hole in the Suncorp Stadium turf, I would have jumped in it then. Playing with Locky showed me that I didn't need to give the stirring speeches of the likes of Cameron Smith to succeed in my new role. So I kept his example in mind as I prepared for my first senior game as a captain.

I was lucky to be supported by an excellent leadership group. Adam Blair, Benji Marshall, Andrew McCullough, Sam Thaiday, Matt Gillett, Ben Hunt, Alex Glenn and Josh McGuire gave me great support throughout 2017, bringing insight and cohesion to our team. We would meet on a regular basis to discuss what the team needed to do in order to play its best, and those players brought ideas that challenged and helped me. I was also lucky to be supported by Alex McKinnon. He knew that I would be appointed captain before I did. When I rang to ask his advice, Macca already had a response prepared: 'Don't think about any possible negatives from this, embrace all that is good about it. You'll be fine.' I'm glad Macca had faith in me because I was uncertain how I would cope with the captaincy. I learnt from our opening matches that there was one key change – you ride the wins and losses much harder as a captain.

The start to my captaincy career wasn't going to be easy – our first four games were against the top four teams from the previous season. We won two of those games and then lost our next game to fall to a 2–3 win–loss record. But then we won six consecutive matches to hit an early groove. That winning streak could easily have crashed in Round 7 when we trailed the Gold Coast Titans at home with only two minutes remaining. Matt Gillett then produced a moment of brilliance, charging down a Titans clearing kick before regathering the ball and finding James Roberts steaming on to a pass. Jimmy ran thirty metres, beating two tackles to score a try that won the game for us.

Sometimes, single moments of brilliance like that can change so much about a season. The media underestimate how small things can lead to big things – if we hadn't stolen that match from the Titans, perhaps we would not have been feeling as good about ourselves and Anthony Milford wouldn't have kicked a 78th-minute field goal to beat the Rabbitohs the following weekend. The media place a lot of importance on which teams win and lose on any given weekend when the truth isn't quite as black and white as that. Usually the best teams aren't playing as well as the media make out and the worst teams aren't playing as badly. The truth is somewhere in between. Winning and losing are contagious. When you're in winning form, you just seem to find ways to keep winning. The aches and pains don't feel as bad during the week and players have a spring in their step at training. When you've had losses, the aches feel worse, and you can develop a feeling in the back of your mind that a loss is still possible even when you're leading.

We ended the six-match winning streak with two consecutive losses and then started another clash with the Rabbitohs in the worst possible way when we dropped the ball from the kick-off. But good teams don't dwell on mistakes. We held the Rabbitohs out in their first attacking set, found our rhythm and won 24–18. I was learning as captain that the support of the senior players around me was important, particularly after two losses in a row. The older players are less likely to let a mistake affect their game – they move on from it and look for new opportunities. That's always a sign that I look for in younger players to see if they have the resilience to bounce back from inevitable mistakes.

I was also learning that, as much as I wanted my actions to have more impact than my words, I still had to talk. I wasn't backward in talking to the team in recent years, but I did that without the responsibility of captaincy. Now there were several times each week when I had to talk to the team: after the traditional captain's run on the day before the game; after the warm-up on game day; and, of course, when we were standing around after conceding a try. That took a while to become part of my routine. And I slowly learnt that there wasn't just one way to talk to all members of the team. Wayne had taught me that in the way he spoke to me in my rookie season. He never shouted at me because he worked out that I didn't need that type of motivation. In my early days as captain, I took a blanket approach to the team. But I soon realised that I had to become more flexible and understanding of the best ways to motivate teammates.

As the Broncos moved strongly through the early part of the season, a storm was brewing on the State of Origin front. It felt like I was in the eye of it as the media began debating whether Billy Slater or I would wear the fullback jersey for Queensland. Billy was back from a shoulder injury for the Storm while I was the incumbent fullback and still playing well. It was a big decision for selectors but I had an easy solution for them – let Billy play fullback. As much as I loved playing in that position, I didn't want the intense scrutiny over whether I should keep my jersey at the expense of Billy. I told Kevin Walters before the team was selected for Origin I that I didn't want to play fullback ahead of Billy. Kevvie told me not to think about it and to leave it with the selectors. I was serious about that because I knew my limitations, and the searing media spotlight – while it had nothing to do with my actions – was still too much for me. The clinic had taught me many coping strategies, but it had also taught me that the best way of coping was to avoid situations that could lead to difficulties. This was one of those times. Unfortunately, I was chosen at fullback ahead of Billy.

The media interest was intense and I understood the reasons for that. I knew how much Billy was loved across Queensland and I knew that I didn't generate the same affection, which was due to my reluctance to tell my story for so long. While I didn't read any articles about the selection, I was aware that it was the major focus of Origin news. Even when you choose to avoid media coverage, you can't escape the big stories. It was obvious from the line of questioning directed at me at media conferences, which I had to do on a weekly basis as Broncos captain. One journalist asked me what it felt like to kill Bambi. I received text messages from well-meaning mates telling me not to worry – which made me worry. I walked into a coffee shop and saw a television playing in the background with commentators arguing about why Billy should play ahead of me. A lovely older lady, moving with the aid of a walking frame, came up to me in a café one lunchtime and told me to ignore all those 'bad things' people were saying about me. And then a federal politician blasted me on radio and social media, saying all sorts of things about my ability as a footballer and insisting he would make an official complaint to the Queensland Rugby League about my selection ahead of Billy. I had never heard of the politician.

I didn't enjoy that Origin camp at all. It was usually my favourite time of the year but this one dragged on. Billy was great about it – he sent me a text before the game, wishing me all the best. That meant a lot to me. Billy and I had been mates for a long time. We had always talked and I was grateful for the things that he did for me. During Origin camp in 2016, when Billy was sidelined with a shoulder reconstruction, he helped me transition into the fullback role for Queensland. His text gave me some confidence but I knew that we faced a serious challenge in Game I. We were without Johnathan

Thurston, Greg Inglis and Matt Scott that night because of injury, but in the end that wasn't the reason for our clunky performance at Suncorp Stadium. The Blues were simply too good that night and surged away for a 28–4 win.

That gave selectors the opportunity to bring back Billy for Game II as we went to Sydney to keep the series alive. J.T. returned from injury but G.I. was still out, leaving a question mark over the make-up of our backline. I was asked to play in the centres for the first time for Queensland. There were questions about my ability to play there as I had only limited experience in that position for my NRL clubs. But I was excited because I had grown up playing in the centres throughout my junior career. It was only in my final year of school that I switched to fullback so I was confident I could play the position, starting inside debutant Valentine Holmes and marking up against Josh Dugan.

There was an air of expectation in Sydney that night after the Blues' big win in Game I. While we had made seven changes, the Blues took in an unchanged squad for the first time in more than twenty years. The celebrations among the crowd started early as the Blues scored three tries in the first half-hour to lead 16–6. That was the scoreline at half-time, leaving us with a clear task: we had to pull back a ten-point deficit in front of a massive Blues home crowd or the series was lost. But I knew that we could do this – we were a winning team and we would find ways to get it done. The Blues had made a habit of losing for some time so I expected that they would be nervous with so much at stake in the second half.

We pegged back some of the Blues' lead in the fifty-third minute when Dane Gagai scored an outstanding try, finishing off a bust by Josh McGuire. The next twenty minutes were an Origin wrestle, until we had a chance with three minutes remaining. On the right side, Michael Morgan sent an inside pass to Dane who stepped off his wing for a try that levelled the scores at 16-all. That left J.T., nursing a shoulder injury, with the task of converting from only a few metres inside the touchline. We had the best man for the moment. The noise was deafening but J.T. set the ball on the tee, adjusted his headgear, walked back a few steps, forgot about the pain in his shoulder and put that ball straight through the middle of the posts.

That was a stirring win in front of a huge Sydney crowd, and it would become my final time on a State of Origin field. With twenty-five minutes to go, I had gone in for a regulation tackle and knocked my thumb on Boyd Cordner's elbow. The knock broke my right thumb, although at the time I had no idea of the damage. I had never broken a bone so I kept playing, hoping that the soreness in my thumb would soon go away. After the game, our team medical staff assessed the injury by asking me to shake hands. I was unable to squeeze and they prepared me for the fact that I had broken my thumb. The next day, I was told I needed surgery, which would keep me out of the Origin decider.

I wasn't selected for the opening Origin match of 2018, which was disappointing. I was hoping that my ten years service would be enough to earn selection for that game, but

I respected the selectors' call. They had a tough job and I knew they wanted to bring in younger players. I decided to announce my retirement from representative football, walking away very grateful and very satisfied with my career. I was approached by selectors to consider playing Game III in 2018, but I didn't want to go back on my retirement announcement.

Sitting on our bench watching the 2017 Origin decider at Suncorp Stadium was a new experience for me. I had played twenty-eight consecutive Origin matches to that point so the flow of the series had become part of my life. I was less nervous playing than watching, but winning that decider was no less exciting. That experience became one of the points I would discuss during my mental health talks. I could have felt many emotions when faced with missing that Origin decider or missing selection for the opening match of 2018. But I had scribbled down the word 'gratitude' so many times since I left the clinic that it had become an entrenched part of my approach to life. Early on in my career, I never dreamt of playing even one Origin match – I really only wanted to play for the Broncos – but not only had I played in twenty-eight consecutive games, I had also won nine of the ten series that I played in. I had the chance to play alongside some of the game's greatest players and to learn from them. For Australia, I had played twenty-three matches and never lost. So, it was easy to be grateful for my representative career. I was a lucky man.

The rest of the 2017 NRL season was a wild ride. Within the space of a few weeks, the Broncos thrashed the Bulldogs, cruised past the Titans 54–0 for the club's largest win on the road, and then gave up 52 points to the Eels at Suncorp Stadium. That left us with another important clash with the Cowboys, this time in Townsville to complete the regular season. We avoided another nail-biter with the Cowboys, winning 20–10 to finish in third place on the ladder, but I hurt my hamstring again in that match. I knew that I would be out for the first week of the finals – a showdown with the second-placed Roosters in Sydney. We lost that match in the final minutes and then returned home in week two to defeat the Panthers. I was proud of the team for reaching a preliminary final against the Storm in Melbourne. My fitness was the subject of plenty of speculation, and Wayne left it to me to decide if I could play. I thought I was ready and took my place at fullback, although I was concerned during the warm-up when I felt a twinge in my hamstring. I tested it again and was convinced that I could play, only for the injury to happen again during the second half. I left the field with thirty minutes remaining as we fell to the Storm 30–0.

That season was one of great promise for the Broncos, but the finals didn't work out for us. If Latrell Mitchell hadn't scored in the final minutes of that qualifying final, we would have received a weekend off and hosted a home preliminary final against the Cowboys – the team we beat comfortably in the final round of the season. But that's how finals football plays out. I finished the year by signing a new four-year deal with the Broncos – I knew it would be the last contract of my career.

My first season as a captain had been eventful – unexpected losses, winning streaks, injuries and near misses. I learnt from all of those experiences and I was a better leader for it. I had the off-season to mend my troublesome hamstrings and to prepare for a 2018 season that would be anything but dull.

CHAPTER 16

A painful goodbye and a joyous arrival

As the 2017 finals series approached, I became increasingly concerned with Nana's health. She had been battling dementia for several years and, while her body was relatively sound, her memory was fading. She had a heavy fall in September 2017 and broke her hip, which caused her plenty of pain and distress. Nana needed surgery to mend the hip but, at age eighty-seven, that operation was always going to be high risk. Nana didn't regain consciousness after her surgery. I sat next to her hospital bed while she lay motionless, hoping that she would make a miraculous recovery. Nana had fought her whole life, overcoming the loss of her only son and husband, but this was a battle she couldn't win.

Nana died days before we played the Melbourne Storm in the preliminary final. I didn't get to say goodbye but I knew that life didn't always give you everything you wanted. If I could have said goodbye, I would have told Nana just how grateful I was for everything she had done for me. I wouldn't have made my way through life without her. As an uncertain teenager, I was desperate for people I could love and trust, who had my best interests at heart. Nana offered all of those things. She was my rock even when my life was a mess. I would ring her before every game I played as part of my pre-game routine. That was always a favourite part of my preparation.

Nana was the subject of the first tattoo that I had commissioned to pay tribute to a family member. I had DELPHINE 29 tattooed on my left wrist. The 29 recognised Nana's birth year of 1929. But this was more of a silent tribute; because I was too scared of her reaction to the tattoo, I kept it hidden from her. I never wanted to make Nana unhappy so it was easier to keep it secret. That wasn't hard because I always strapped my wrist when I played, and I started wearing long sleeves when I saw Nana. One day, she caught a glimpse of the tattoo and asked: 'What's that thing on your wrist, Darius?' I told her it was nothing and quickly changed the subject. Nana eventually found out about the tattoo from one of her friends who had read something in the papers about it. Nana was chuffed. She thought it was brilliant, so I needn't have worried about her reaction.

The tattoo of Nana's name was the second that I had done, following a BRONCOS PREMIERS '06 tattoo on my left bicep. Then followed a series of tattoos associated with my family, footy and inspiration following my stay at the clinic. Each one represented something meaningful to me and included:

- the initials of my uncle Dallyn and my grandfather Herbie on either side of my right Achilles
- Q166 on my left hip to recognise my selection as the 166th player to represent Queensland in State of Origin
- an eagle on my left shoulder as a sign of strength
- BOYD above my belly button to honour my family name
- DRAGONS PREMIERS 2010 on my right rib cage
- WCC2011 on my left tricep to acknowledge the Dragons' World Club Challenge win
- a relaxing image of a beach and a palm tree on my left shoulder around the eagle tattoo
- KAYLA on my right forearm, later surrounded by a dragon and roses
- PROVE YOUR STRENGTH, LET COURAGE SHINE, DON'T GIVE INTO WEAKNESS, NEVER BACK DOWN plus doves on my right arm
- a long message, on my left calf, after I left the clinic in 2014: YOU GAIN STRENGTH, COURAGE AND CONFIDENCE BY EVERY EXPERIENCE IN WHICH YOU REALLY STOP TO LOOK FEAR IN THE FACE. YOU ARE ABLE TO SAY TO YOURSELF 'I HAVE LIVED THROUGH THIS HORROR'. I CAN TAKE THE NEXT THING THAT COMES ALONG. YOU MUST DO THE THINGS YOU THINK YOU CANNOT DO.

- Chinese symbols on my spine which reflect: EVEN WHEN I LOSE I'M WINNING
- STRONG, CONFIDENT, FEARLESS across my chest, a few months after leaving the clinic
- K and our wedding date in Roman numerals on my left ring finger
- WILLOW and her birthdate on the back of my left calf
- a semicolon near my left thumb to signify that there is no full stop in life – it always keeps going
- GRATITUDE on my right wrist in 2017.

The final tattoo that I received has a long backstory. Kayla and I tried for a long time to have a second child. Our marriage had become as stable and as rewarding as we had ever experienced. We still had our challenging moments. It's impossible not to have that when you have two people in a marriage who are so competitive. But we had also learnt to become patient with each other – far more patient than we had been a few years earlier. Willow had helped with that. She was growing into the most dear little girl that I had ever known. I couldn't describe the emotions that she stirred within me. I could see in her traits of the only family that I knew. Willow had Nana's determination; she had Kayla's sharp mind and her love of life; and she had an outgoing nature that clearly didn't come from me. When Willow had reached the adorable age of eighteen months, Kayla and I began to try for a little sister or brother. We thought that this would be as straightforward as it had been in early

2015 when Kayla's pregnancy shocked us. But this wasn't to be.

After trying for more than a year to fall pregnant, Kayla began to worry that a second child may not happen for us. It wasn't an easy time. I wanted a large family because I had never known that growing up. My own limited memories of family life ended early when my uncle Dallyn and grandfather passed away, and then Mum battled with her mental health. The clinic taught me the importance of family. During my troubled times, I had football ranked first, second and third in my life. There really was nothing else. That focus changed once I left the clinic, and it was reinforced when Willow was born. It's impossible not to see life differently when kids arrive.

Kayla began to focus on her blossoming entrepreneurial career. She had begun a blog in 2015, building a strong audience that enjoyed her honest insights into life as a mum, wife and social media influencer. While I avoided social media at all costs, Kayla enjoyed her social media platforms. In 2018, she began a series of live events based around empowering women to overcome life's struggles. These events were very successful due to Kayla's drive and determination. She knew how to achieve her goals.

That helped to take Kayla's mind off our struggles to fall pregnant. We basically gave up on the idea of having a second child, deciding that we had wanted it so badly that it was only adding to the stress to conceive. It was a very painful and stressful time but made us both stronger. It is something we have put behind us now. Early in 2019, Kayla began to feel tired and unwell, which she attributed to her busy schedule as a mum with a growing business. One particular day we took Willow to the beach on the Gold Coast but lasted only a short time before Kayla felt too unwell to stay there. On our way back home to Brisbane, Kayla asked me to stop at a chemist so that she could buy a pregnancy test. She was doing this simply to rule out pregnancy as the reason for her illness, knowing that we had been unable to fall pregnant after eighteen months of trying. I was in the shower at home when Kayla came into the bathroom to tell me that the pregnancy test had revealed the most unlikely news – she was pregnant again.

This pregnancy was greeted in a very different fashion from our first. We both cried at the surprise and the excitement of having a sibling for Willow. I took this as a sign that our marriage had progressed to a point where Kayla was confident that this baby would come into a family that was together for the long term. After a few months, we learnt that we would be blessed with another little girl, so we began to prepare a very excited Willow for the arrival of her new sister.

The arrival of our little girl was very different from the calm birth of Willow. More than three weeks before the due date, Kayla thought she had gone into labour. We went to the hospital but were told that it was a false alarm and there was nothing to worry about. That night, as Kayla and I were lying in bed and I was laughing with her for being worried about going into labour, Kayla's waters broke. Had there ever been a time when a husband had been proven so wrong? We hadn't prepared a thing for the hospital so we rushed to get

Kayla's bag packed, transferring a sleeping Willow to the car before we headed in. It was to prove a long night because the birth was anything but straightforward. The baby's heart rate began to surge as Kayla's labour became difficult. It was a scary time. In the end, Kayla underwent emergency caesarean surgery to bring our new little girl into the world. Romi Yvés Boyd was born on 28 September 2019 at 7.40 a.m. She had arrived three weeks early, a sister to a very proud and excited Willow, who had celebrated her fourth birthday only a few days earlier.

That final tattoo was 'ROMI' on my left shoulder blade. I had cried as soon as I held her, overcome with the emotion of Romi's arrival as well as Kayla emerging safely from a draining night. She had been incredible, as always, and she bonded with Romi immediately. There was some sadness that my Nana would not get to meet Romi. She had seen Willow grow to her first birthday and I had happy memories of their brief time together. Nana had taught me all I knew about family and I would always tell our daughters of their great-grandmother and what family meant to her.

Kayla and I were now busy with a house that buzzed with Willow's energy and Romi's needs as a newborn. Some of our friends were also welcoming new arrivals. The most joyous of those was Alex and Teigan McKinnon's baby girl Harriet, who was born in October 2018. I didn't need to pass on any tips about parenting to Macca – he always seemed to have everything under control. Harriet arrived twelve months after Macca and Teigan were married in a ceremony that was incredibly moving. I was honoured to be Macca's best man and part of their bridal party that included Kayla and my Queensland teammate Dane Gagai. Macca was adamant that he wanted to stand throughout the ceremony and that was never in doubt. It was one of the most emotional events I had witnessed.

My best man duties included making a speech at the reception. I wanted to be as open as I could because that had always been the mark of the friendship between Macca and me. You always felt you could be yourself around Macca. I wasn't confident enough to speak off the cuff, so I read my speech. Here's how it went:

Good evening. Thanks so much to Alex and Teigan for this wonderful day. I have been lucky to know Alex and Teigan for many years – there has always been something very special about them and today's ceremony brought all of that together. It was a privilege to be part of it. I'll pay my own tribute to the bridesmaids – yes, I'm biased but they are stunning.

I'll go back to the start of my friendship with Macca. It all began in a house shared by young rugby league players. That sounds like the start of a disaster movie but here we are today, Macca. It's all turned out fine. Macca and I met about eight years ago when we were both playing at the Dragons. One of our roommates moved out. We needed another roommate and along came Macca. I was a different person back then. I wasn't great at meeting new people. I had a small group of friends and I wasn't really that open to new mates.

But how do you not become friends with Macca? And, we struck gold with Macca the housemate. The Dragons paid for his rent so he was never behind. He'd been to boarding school so he brought a strict discipline into the house. If we went out, he would drive. How good was this bloke? He even helped with the shopping and he was extremely well mannered. Teigan, no wonder you snapped him up.

Not long after, my then girlfriend Kayla moved in with Macca and me. Soon after, we came to know Teigan. She was very quiet at first. And she was pretty young. As Kayla would say, Teigan was an 'old soul'. She was very wise. Just like Macca – they were not your typical teenagers.

We both went from the Dragons to Newcastle and we moved into our own places then.

A lot of people have asked me over the years what Macca was like as a teammate. I tell them he was a bloody good housemate but an even better teammate. He always gave his best. He worked his backside off on the field. He would be the guy who never stopped trying. Ask Wayne Bennett – he took Macca from the Dragons to the Knights with him because Wayne would love a team of Alex McKinnons.

I don't talk much about my emotions or feelings. But Macca asks about them. He's one of the few blokes I would talk to about that. Even when he had his problems, he was still asking questions about me. He became a very close mate of mine. When Alex was in his darkest times a few years back, he still had that Macca smile. He was still positive. He had that influence on others. I still don't know if Macca knows the impact he has on other people. We were worried for him – he was more worried for his mates.

Many of us here tonight got to know of the amazing relationship between Macca and Teigan. If there was one positive to come out of Macca's accident, it's that many people around the country got to know just how special this couple are. They have been together for a long time and they have such a future ahead of them. Thanks for asking Kayla and me to be a part of your wedding. We wish you all the best for the years to come.

CHAPTER 17

Wayne rides off

THERE WAS NO OTHER WAY TO REMEMBER 2018 THAN THE year that the Broncos and Wayne Bennett split. It was the end of a marriage that was once the tightest in football, before a shock separation in 2008. Wayne and the Broncos got back together again in 2015 but it was clear by the start of 2018 that divorce was coming. And this time there would be no reconciliation.

The speculation about Wayne's future began early in 2018 with criticism in the media of our start to the season. Wayne's contract wasn't up until the end of 2019, but that was close enough for journalists to begin speculating on who might fill the Broncos coaching position. The media were chasing this story because it featured two of the most reliable ingredients for reader interest: Wayne Bennett and the Broncos. Our Broncos communications team explained that any story on a news website with the words 'Wayne

Bennett' and 'Broncos' helped to attract online traffic. So, even though we won three of our opening six games, the pressure on Wayne was building. Initially, the Broncos were strongly linked in media reports to Cowboys coach Paul Green, although I'm not sure the club ever reached out to him. These stories were all based on speculation so it wasn't hard for the media to toss up a bunch of names as contenders. After Paul re-signed with the Cowboys, the media moved on to Melbourne Storm coach Craig Bellamy as the next target. And Craig helped to ramp up the interest in that story when he admitted he was open to other offers once his Storm contract expired.

The rumours were impossible for the playing group to ignore. Some of us didn't read them but some players did, so that meant that the whole group quickly became aware of them. But it was all speculation to us, because the club had told us that Wayne had a contract until the end of 2019 that would be honoured. Wayne was always very good at keeping outside news away from the playing group. He wanted us to focus on our season rather than on stories that we couldn't control. So, in the early months of the 2018 season, we trucked along as a playing group without getting caught up in the coaching rumours.

As part of my role as captain, I met regularly with our CEO Paul White. Like me, Whitey had featured previously on the ABC's *Australian Story*. His episode focused on his battle with a brain tumour that was inoperable, which Whitey fought with large doses of chemotherapy, radiation and sheer courage. We knew that he was made of tough stuff. The father of four girls, Whitey played for Souths in Brisbane – Wayne's old club – before his work as a police officer took him to rural and regional towns. Whitey was the captain-coach of most bush teams that he played in, achieving representative honours and developing a reputation for toughness and fairness. Whitey became the most senior police officer in Mount Isa, where he was highly regarded for his work in a community that faced plenty of challenges. He showed incredible fight to continue working as Broncos CEO throughout his cancer treatment. Some weeks he struggled as the chemotherapy knocked him around. But Whitey was always positive, always passionate and very popular among staff.

The relationship between Whitey and Wayne went back more than thirty years to when they were both at the police academy – Wayne as a leader and Whitey as a recruit. They had plenty in common outside football and policing. Both were born and raised in regional areas of Queensland. Both were devoted to their families. Both had a good sense of humour. And both were committed to excellence. Their relationship had grown over the decades and Wayne had been publicly supportive of Whitey's appointment as Broncos CEO in 2010. Whitey was a key figure in bringing Wayne back to the club in 2015.

But that became history in 2018 as their relationship broke down over the Broncos' future. Behind the scenes, the Broncos had invited Wayne to move into a coaching director role as part of a long-term contract that would keep him at the Broncos. Wayne told the club he wasn't interested in that offer – he wanted to stay head coach. The media interest intensified. You can only understand the true force of a media storm when you're in the middle of it. It's hard to explain it to someone who has been fortunate enough to escape the intense concentration of a media pack, when photographers hide outside your house or your place of work. It feels as though you can never get away from it. This story had reached that level of intensity. It's part of life in rugby league, but that doesn't mean that it's easy to handle.

Fortunately, Whitey and Wayne were calm and ultra professional in how they treated me during this time. As captain, I was caught in the middle. I had enormous respect for Wayne and Whitey. I found both men honourable and I hoped that they could find common ground in the negotiations. On behalf of the players, I spoke with Wayne and Whitey to learn more about the coaching negotiations. There was very little that either could tell me in terms of how it would play out – they were continuing discussions and they promised to keep me updated with any relevant details. Whitey told me that the Broncos realised that some of the best coaches in the NRL were all coming off contract at the same time and, if they delayed any move, they could miss out on testing the market to see which coach may be best for Brisbane while Wayne moved into a coaching director role.

On the field, we struggled to find rhythm across the year. Our longest winning streak was three matches. Our longest losing streak was two matches. Just when we thought we were on a roll, we would drop a game. In Round 18, we struggled in a poor 26–6 loss to the Warriors at Suncorp Stadium. The following week, we put 50 points on Penrith. It was that type of season. We had some great moments – we piled on two tries in the final five minutes to stun the Sydney Roosters at home in Round 11. One of those tries came from a special moment when James Roberts simply ran around the Roosters with blistering pace in the same way a fast Under 8s player runs around his opposition. This was life with a young team. We had lost Benji Marshall, Adam Blair and Ben Hunt in the off-season, which made a noticeable change to the leadership group. We welcomed in a bunch of young players, including the athletic Payne Haas. He made his debut in Round 8 with statistics that made him a potential star: eighteen years old, 194 centimetres, 120 kilograms and genuinely fast. By the end of the season, we welcomed another promising young forward in David Fifita who had started the year in suburban Under 18s. His stats and speed were similar to Payne's.

In Round 12, Wayne recorded his eight-hundredth game as coach – he was the first man to do that – but the milestone was not silencing the debate on Brisbane's coaching future. When we lost to the Storm in Melbourne in Round 14, the post-match questions for Craig Bellamy revolved around whether he would take up a rumoured offer to join the Broncos for the 2019 season. But the moment that the story really seemed to escalate came after our Round 22 loss to the Cowboys in Townsville. Later that weekend would be Whitey's annual barbecue for all the Broncos' staff and players. Whitey held the event at his house to thank everyone for their efforts for the club. Given the tension over the coaching uncertainty, Wayne decided he wouldn't go to the barbecue. Our flight home was delayed and a few players decided at Townsville Airport that before going to Whitey's place they would duck around to Wayne's place as a sign of support for the coach. This wasn't about choosing between one barbecue or another, it was simply support for both sides of the coaching debate. I texted Whitey the next day to let him know that I would be among several players dropping into Wayne's place that night. Whitey was fine with that and the night seemed to work out well for everyone.

But the media learnt of the duelling barbecues and they couldn't resist the story. All of a sudden, the debate about the Broncos' coaching future descended into a story about who had a steak at whose place on a Saturday night. It was a difficult position for the players to be in, but most understood that the situation was no one's fault. It was purely the business of rugby league. Two weeks later, I was asked at a press conference about the barbecues and if I wanted Wayne to stay on for the next season. I told journalists: 'He's one of the best coaches in the competition so I think, as long as he's motivated and wanting to coach, he definitely deserves an opportunity.'

Whitey and Wayne appreciated that players were caught in the middle so they treated us professionally at all times. I don't believe the uncertainty affected our season as we struggled for consistency, finishing sixth on the ladder. We hosted the Dragons in a sudden-death clash in the first week of the finals and we were thrashed 48–18. We had led 10–2 but the Dragons raced home in a result that increased the speculation about the Broncos' coaching future. It was a disappointing end to a season that could have delivered a lot more. The Roosters won the premiership but we had beaten them twice that season. We also beat the Sharks and Rabbitohs who had top-four positions.

We went into our off-season unsure if Wayne would coach us in the next season, but the playing group received a text message from him on 25 September: 'I'm committed to you for 2019 and excited with what we can achieve together. Have a good rest for us to have the best possible season. Have a fire in the belly for 2019. Coach'

That news was well received by the playing group but this story was a long way from over. We returned to training in November with the media now openly reporting that the Broncos and South Sydney were looking to swap Wayne and their coach Anthony Seibold for the 2019 season. I had met Seibs during his time as an assistant coach with the Queensland Origin team, but I didn't know him well. Seibs had been named the Dally M Coach of the Year for his work with the Rabbitohs in 2018 – his first year as a head NRL coach following an apprenticeship that included time in Melbourne. He had done a great job with the Bunnies and he was the man that the Broncos wanted. The prospect of Wayne seeing out his 2019 contract was not likely because the relationship between him and Whitey and most of the Broncos board had fractured beyond repair.

The media reports reached saturation level. I wasn't reading the papers but the story was inescapable – everyone was talking about it. We were a few weeks into pre-season training when Wayne called a meeting of all players on Friday, 30 November. I expected that Wayne would tell us that he was leaving and that Seibs would be our new coach. Instead, he told us he would definitely coach throughout 2019 and that he was looking forward to the season with us. Wayne told us that the only reason he wouldn't be coaching us would be if the Broncos sacked him, and he wasn't sure if that would happen. It was a head-spinning day. I later texted Wayne, telling him: 'I'm glad you're staying, Coach.'

Two days later, the relationship between Wayne and the Broncos reached the end. At a press conference on Sunday afternoon, 2 December, Whitey announced that Wayne had been sacked by the Broncos and that Seibs would coach our club in 2019 and beyond. I didn't have much time to get my head around the news. Seibs rang me that night for a chat and told me that he would start immediately by running a training session the following morning with the coaching staff that he brought with him to Brisbane. Forget the saying that a week is a long time in football – in one weekend I said goodbye to the coach who had been there for my whole NRL career. Wayne was signed by Souths and moved into his new role immediately.

There was no chance I would follow Wayne to South Sydney. Brisbane was my home and I was staying with the club that meant the most to me. The events of 2018 hadn't been good for anyone – no one involved enjoyed the process. But, if I had learnt anything from my stay at the clinic and the years that followed, it was that there would always be challenges in life. I didn't spend any time thinking about who was to blame for the events of the past nine months or so. They happened and now everyone involved had to make the best of the outcomes. I still respected Wayne and Whitey, and I felt for them both.

This would be the start of the next chapter in my friendship with Wayne. We had gone through a few phases. In 2006 I was too shy to start conversations with him. I was petrified Wayne would criticise me in his weekly player assessments. He continued those assessments right through our time together, only making a slight change to the process in all of those years, by asking players to rate their own match performance out of ten before he gave each player his verdict in front of the playing group. I always gave my mark on the low side.

Our relationship changed when I came out of the clinic. I opened up and spoke to Wayne more. That's when our friendship became more mature. I didn't always listen to Wayne when I was younger but the wisdom he tried to impart in 2006 was still relevant thirteen years later. I could have asked him for a lot more help and advice in my younger days but I was often confused and I didn't know what help I needed.

I learnt a lot about people just by observing Wayne. People may think that he doesn't smile much or crack jokes but he is always ready for a laugh. Wayne was happy to bring up the popular gag about his resemblance to Hollywood legend Clint Eastwood. He loved players like Willie Mason, Sam Thaiday and Wendell Sailor – guys who were completely different from him. He would pull up a chair near them and listen and laugh. He was brilliant at getting the most out of his players by knowing how to treat them as individuals.

We won two premierships together and a World Club Challenge, moved clubs together three times and qualified for the finals eleven times in thirteen seasons. But that's not why I'm grateful to Wayne. I would have gone off the rails without him. Early on in my career, I had few people who I could trust completely, but Wayne was one of them. When I went to the clinic, Wayne supported me at every step. He never asked when I would be back playing footy, knowing that I could not rush back. He visited me at the clinic and I told him more during that visit than I had told him during our previous eight years together. Wayne selflessly let me find my way back when I was ready to play again. I can never repay him.

There was a time when I couldn't have contemplated playing for another NRL coach. But I viewed Wayne's departure as a chance to learn something from a new coach. That was another sign of my progress in life. I was captain and I needed to build a relationship with the new coach to ensure the best outcome for the Broncos. As we headed into Christmas 2018, I was looking forward to the final years of my footy career.

CHAPTER 18

A new coach

ANTHONY SEIBOLD AND I HAD PLENTY IN COMMON: WE SET high standards; we avoided reading media stories; and we had loved rugby league since we were young. Seibs had played for the Broncos in reserve grade before making his first-grade debut for the Canberra Raiders in a team featuring legends such as Ricky Stuart, Laurie Daley and Bradley Clyde. He chose footy despite excelling as a young cricketer, playing alongside the likes of future Australian star Andrew Symonds in Queensland schoolboy teams. His rugby league journey took him to the United Kingdom as a player and later as an assistant coach before he returned to Australia to develop his coaching career.

Seibs was also a teacher by profession and those skills were obvious as he took over a team that welcomed him from the first day. With an attention to detail, he began looking for every possible angle to improve his new club. He analysed data in ways that I hadn't seen, crunching statistics from training sessions to understand the best ways that we could prepare for the season ahead. Through this research Seibs had benchmarked the physical intensity of an average NRL game and he could check the stats from our training sessions to compare our exertion. He wanted us to train at an intensity higher than an NRL game, so he continued to work us hard through the pre-season. Seibs left very little to chance, even analysing the average ages of each NRL squad to get a better understanding of where the Broncos ranked on all types of comparisons. We were the youngest squad in the competition.

Seibs had clearly been soaking up information about footy for years in much the same way that I had. But he was relaxed away from the field and easy to speak with. I enjoyed learning his approach and collaborating with him on the season ahead. This situation did not spark the adjustment disorder that had been diagnosed at the clinic. Yes, the routine from my thirteen years in the NRL was gone but I had plenty of time to get used to a new schedule before the season started. I was excited at the prospect of learning new things and challenging my perspectives on footy. I was impressed with Seibs' desire to learn as much as he could about our playing group and I was looking forward to working with him as a captain.

We knew that the scrutiny on the Broncos would be more intense than ever as we started the season, although my view about the road ahead was clearly different from the media's. In a competition as tough and as even as the NRL, it was a huge ask to expect a young team to adapt to a new playing style under a new coach and have instant success. That's not an excuse – the Broncos have never made excuses and never will – but it's likely that changes can take time to adapt. We had farewelled two of our most experienced forwards at the end of 2018 – Sam Thaiday had retired and Josh McGuire had moved to the Cowboys, along with outside backs Jordan Kahu and Tom Opacic.

We were slow off the mark with a Round 1 loss to the Storm in Melbourne, but we returned home with a comfortable win over the Cowboys which raised the excitement levels. Then four consecutive losses, including a 36–4 result against the Roosters, ignited the media criticism under Seibs. By Round 6, we were a club in 'crisis' according to media reports. Former players were already calling for Seibs to be sacked.

We defeated Cronulla in Round 7 and then lined up against South Sydney for my three-hundredth NRL match. I never got too worked up by milestone games, but my three hundredth did mean something to me. I was grateful for all the luck that had fallen my way over the years to enable me to reach three hundred games because I knew plenty of players didn't have the same luck. The Broncos secretly invited my high school coach, Rod Patison, to present the jersey for my three-hundredth match in an informal ceremony at the club. It was a great surprise. Rod had retired from teaching three years earlier but he would always be one of the most influential people in my early career. Having him join me for that moment was special.

I received a lot of interview requests because my milestone game would be my first club game against a team coached by Wayne. That was a nice coincidence but it wasn't something that I got emotional about – it wasn't like Wayne and I were marking each other in the game. But I was pleased that Wayne would be there because I owed so much of my career to him. He had been at the three-hundredth matches of other players whom he had coached since they were rookies – Darren Lockyer, Sam Thaiday and Corey Parker among them – and I knew that he wanted to be at my three hundredth, so the fact that we were playing the Rabbitohs saved him a trip. Wayne's team got the better of us that night in a 38–6 outcome that increased the pressure on our team.

The game against the Rabbitohs marked the debut of our halfback Tom Dearden only a few months after his eighteenth birthday. Tommy had gone to my old school Palm Beach Currumbin High so I had kept an eye out for him since he signed with the Broncos. He was another example of the burst of youth that seemed to be infiltrating most clubs. These players were very different from me when I came into the NRL at eighteen. The likes of David Fifita and Payne Haas were fitter, faster and stronger than any young player I played with in junior systems. Today's teenagers get the best of the best at a younger age. School rugby league programs take in plenty of elements that they have learnt from NRL clubs. I learnt a lot during my time at Palm Beach Currumbin High but the school's program wasn't then modelled on NRL systems. Add these advances including improved science, technology, diets and supplements and it's no wonder that the NRL seems to be getting younger.

That doesn't mean it's easier to choose the players of the future. Recruitment managers still need to roll the dice on which young players will be good enough for the NRL. The difficulties in transitioning from being a junior to a senior star were shown when the NRL had an Under 20 competition. About 90 per cent of players did not graduate to the NRL. This is not an easy game to build a career in, even if you're an eighteen-year-old with enormous strength, speed and fitness. There are still intangible elements that make our game so demanding.

One of the key factors in determining which younger players are cut out for an NRL career is their defensive abilities. It's easier to stand out playing in age-group footy than it is against grown men. That's why we sometimes saw big scorelines in NRL Under 20 matches. Every time you step up a level, so does the defensive intensity. A veteran Queensland Cup player will have the experience and the smarts to provide a rising teenage star with a reality check if they're not quite up to standard.

If a young player can jump through those hoops, then they need the mental toughness to cope with a career in the spotlight. That's when social media becomes a factor. When I was a young player, social media wasn't an issue. There was no Twitter, Instagram or Snapchat. Facebook was a baby without much reach. But social media became massive and developed an ability to seriously impact the mental health of athletes who could not handle its negativity. There can be so much hatred, particularly from a footy fan who is upset about something that's happened in a game. I know that firsthand – it's one of the reasons that I made a conscious decision not to be on social media. Reading post after post of criticism directed at me is not good for my mental health. So I avoid it. On social media, everyone knows how to play. Everyone knows how to coach. They know how to set defensive structures. They know how to beat defensive structures. They know how to devise attacking systems. And they know how to shut down attacking systems. Social media has all the answers; unfortunately, they arrive after games have finished. Players usually know if they have played well. They don't need to go to social media to get an opinion that they can get from their teammates, their coach or their trusted friends.

As someone who is not on social media, I realise that I'm in the minority. So I have spoken to Kayla and my teammates about using and understanding the different platforms because there are many positives that can come from them. But it's important for young players to understand that people show the best sides of themselves on social media. It's not always a true and accurate reflection of what is going on in their lives. Few show their down times or their challenges. If you compare your life to the lives that people present on social media, you're always going to be worse off. Young people don't always understand that.

Our young Broncos squad had to be wary on social media as our 2019 season fluctuated from excellent wins to frustrating losses. We strung together three consecutive wins from Round 9 but followed that with three consecutive losses. With a finals spot on the line, we won three of our last five matches to seal eighth place with a record of eleven wins, one draw and twelve losses. Given all we had been through over the last twelve months, I was proud of the team for making the finals and excited at the thought of what we could do during September. We would play Parramatta in an elimination final in Sydney, two weeks after we defeated them at Suncorp Stadium.

There was nothing at training that week to suggest the disaster that was to unfold on a Sunday afternoon against Parramatta. We trained well and we had every reason to think that we would be hard to beat. But that all unravelled within minutes of the elimination final. Parramatta scored eleven tries to win 58–0, making it the heaviest loss in Broncos history. We tried desperately on the field to change momentum. The early discussions behind the goalposts were about fixing the defensive errors that had let Parramatta in for early tries. After the scoreline got beyond our reach, there wasn't much left to say behind the posts – we just had to put our heads down and pull back as many points as possible.

The reaction was as severe as I can remember after any game. I could only imagine the social media meltdown, but I knew from teammates that it was vicious. The next day's 'Mad Monday' gathering was relatively flat as the shock of the loss gave way to the reality of our disappointing end to the season. I knew that Seibs would work extra hard after the game to understand how a team that defeated Parramatta two weeks earlier lost so badly. He asked me to his house on Tuesday to discuss the loss and the next steps for the club. Seibs was up front – he was taking the captaincy from me. He told me that he wanted to take the pressure off me and enable me to play without that responsibility. He also wanted to move me to the centres. I would always do what the coach wanted, without question, because I knew that he was doing what he considered best for the team. That was my approach. I told Seibs, though, that I would have liked to retain the captaincy because I had enjoyed it over the last three seasons. I hadn't known what to expect when I took on the role but I'd gained a lot of satisfaction from helping younger players, trying to repay the favours that were given to me when I was a teenager at the Broncos.

My time at the clinic had prepared me well for a moment like this. The clinic had convinced me to focus more on family than football, and our house was full of excitement at the prospect of Romi's arrival in the coming weeks. Kayla had never looked more beautiful as she entered the final stage of her pregnancy, while Willow was bouncing at the prospect of meeting her new sister. Yes, the Broncos had lost 58–0 and that hurt deeply, but it was left at the front door of our house. There was no point dwelling on it and sulking – I had done that for many years and it didn't get me far. I wanted to enjoy my time with my family as we awaited Romi's arrival. At the same time, I would prepare to resume training and ensure I was in a good mindset to do that.

My stint as Broncos' captain was over. But rugby league had given me so much. If I had told my younger self that I would have the chance to captain just one game for the team I had grown up supporting, I would have taken that opportunity in a heartbeat. As your career goes on, you can fall into a trap of wanting more and more. Sometimes, you should simply give thanks for what's been achieved. Considering the average NRL career was forty-two games, I had so much to appreciate. And I had a chance the next season to take a further step with a young group that took enormous strides in a year that promised to shape them.

CHAPTER 19

Calling it a day

You only retire once.

That's what I kept telling myself as I prepared for a media conference in March 2020 to announce that I would be playing one last NRL season. I had known some teammates who had retired and returned to play again, but this was going to be it for me. I knew that for certain. I had made my decision about a month earlier, on a hot Brisbane night as Kayla and I had dinner with George Mimis. George has always had a way of making me think about things in different ways. I was having a rare glass of wine when he asked if 2020 was going to be my last season. That was the lightbulb moment for me. It wasn't like I hadn't thought about the end of my career, but that one question began to crystallise the decision for me. I told George that I wasn't sure, so he asked me in a different way: 'What's going to make you play on in 2021? What are the reasons?'

I thought about it that night and into the next few days. I had enjoyed my best off-season with our young family – Romi was a blessing, and she and Willow continued to fill Kayla and I with joy at home. I still had a contract for 2021, but that wasn't a significant factor for me. I simply weighed up the reasons for playing on in 2021 versus the reasons for retiring after 2020. The reasons for retiring won out. There were simply more of them. Retiring would give me certainty about the next chapter of my life. I could start to plan for the next stage knowing that my professional sports career would end later that year. I would be able to transition into a new chapter free of a pre-season schedule, free of rigorous training routines, club commitments and gym sessions. I could make plans that professional athletes couldn't make. That certainty was attractive to me.

I hadn't stopped enjoying football. Playing well and winning with the Broncos was still just as important to me as it had been in my fourteen previous seasons. In fact, I don't remember starting a season so keen to win a premiership. The pre-season had some bright moments. I was topping the fitness tests across the Broncos squad. I may have been the oldest player but I could still record solid fitness numbers. That had a lot to do with the fact that I was on my fifteenth pre-season, which gave me a head start on some teammates. And I remained committed to my normal standards.

The pre-season wasn't smooth. I had changed my diet over summer after watching an American TV documentary that followed elite athletes as they ate diets free of animal products. They produced a compelling case of how their physical performance had improved on the new diet. I wasn't totally convinced but I knew that I was getting older, so I was always looking for an advantage in my fitness. I found the diet easy to follow but it was having an unexpected impact on my body. I was losing up to four kilograms each day at training. I would leave home weighing at least ninety-three kilograms and return at about eighty-nine. I hadn't been so light since my first NRL season when my eighteen-year-old body was still getting used to a full weights program. That concerned me, but I shouldn't have been surprised. The combination of a reduction in protein, a demanding pre-season program and the sticky Brisbane summer meant that I was struggling to retain weight. So, I would come home and start the serious task of putting weight on before I went to bed. And it was hard work – protein shakes, big meals and whatever else I could find. It was lucky that I liked cooking.

A few of my Broncos teammates had also watched the documentary and decided to experiment with the diet, although I'm not sure they were as dedicated to the change. I would have struggled to stick with it at the same age. The media heard about the diet and their reports made it sound as though I was the Pied Piper leading the young Broncos from the butcher's shop into the fruit and vegetable stand. That wasn't the case, but it made for a good story.

Like any other element of my footballing life, I followed the diet to the letter. But I knew I couldn't keep it up. Just before Christmas, we had some friends over for a barbecue and I couldn't resist a steak. It tasted superb. Yep, I needed more of that. I was immediately back in the fold, and I knew it was the best thing for my football. Because I didn't read newspapers, I wasn't aware that I was still being written up as a 'vegan' for at least six weeks afterwards, and that it was apparently affecting my chances of retaining my first-grade position. I managed to correct the record before our first trial game of the summer, at least ensuring I wouldn't have spectators shouting over the fence for me to eat a steak.

So, my fifteenth and final pre-season had been eventful. I had lost the captaincy, experimented with a diet unsuited to a Brisbane summer and was surrounded by constant speculation over my place in the team. But my decision to retire had nothing to do with those matters. I had weighed it up and made the decision for myself. I was proud of that fact. Of course, I had valued Kayla's thoughts and George's guidance because they had been along most of the journey with me. But this was a decision that I made and owned weeks before I told the Broncos. That gave my decision a chance to settle and for me to make sure it was right. As the weeks went on, I felt surer of the decision, to the point of excitement.

I decided to make the announcement on Friday, 6 March – one week before our season began. On the previous Tuesday, I sat down separately with Anthony Seibold and Paul White to tell them about my decision. As I expected, they were fabulous. Seibs and Whitey wanted to sit alongside me at my media conference. I was glad that they would be there. But I kept the news quiet from my teammates until after our season launch on the Thursday night. After the launch, I put some words on the players' message group to tell them I would be announcing my retirement at 8 a.m. the next day. I was blown away by their good wishes.

Then, I sat down and wrote a letter that set out the reasons for my retirement. I was happy for this letter to be published widely to give the reasons for my decision in my own words. I planned to read it out at the start of my media conference and then to take questions. It had been a long time since I had handwritten a letter. I wanted to get it down on one page, but that was never going to happen. Three pages, 545 words and one tired hand later, I was finished. I had summed up everything that I wanted to say. Here's how it read:

I don't remember the first time I was told I would play in the National Rugby League. I was eighteen years old, everything was happening at a crazy speed and everything was new.

But I do remember the time that I decided that my NRL career would end. I was at dinner last month when a friend asked me if this would be my last season. It had been in the back of my mind, but that one question made it feel urgent. And, I knew right then that this would be it. There were more reasons why it should be my last season rather than why it shouldn't.

So, now it's time to tell you that news. This 2020 season will be my last in rugby league. I have another season to give. My body feels great, I'm still excited about playing. But I'm also excited about the next chapter of my life. And I will go into that next chapter so grateful for everything that has happened over my fifteen seasons in the NRL.

Rugby league cops a lot of criticism but only a game like rugby league could have provided the journey that I've had on and off the field. Rugby league helped me out of my dark times. The game provided the support I needed as I sought help to improve my mental health. And the game has provided the platform for me to tell that story to others. I'll always be grateful for that.

I met my incredible wife Kayla while I was playing rugby league. What a journey we've had together. We now have two beautiful daughters. Our family brings me happiness I can't describe. I am so grateful for that.

I have met some incredible people along the way. People who have helped me grow from a shy, introverted kid to a very happy, proud and compassionate man. Those people know who they are and I will always value them.

For my teammates, coaches, club staff and my management team – I can never thank you enough. I've been fortunate to have some great times in footy – a premiership in my first year with the Broncos, a premiership at the Dragons, State of Origin series wins that will stay with me forever, and the honour of playing for my country. I grew up a Broncos supporter and I was lucky enough to captain this great club. But you can only do those things because of teammates, coaches and management. I'm grateful for them all.

I'll miss competing, I'll miss the victories and I'll miss sharing the journey with teammates. But, most of all, I'll miss the good wishes of the fans who make rugby league possible. Yes, I've copped criticism over the years but I've received far more good wishes than bad. The support of fans has meant a lot to me. It's always humbling to think of the person who saves every cent to buy a ticket to watch their team. They're the foundation of this game.

I'll join those fans after the 2020 season as I stay involved in this great game. I owe rugby league a lot. It's been very good to me. And I will forever be grateful for that.

My sincere thanks

Darius Boyd

I finished off writing about the fans because that's what I started as in rugby league and it's what I would always be. I'm a fan of rugby league in so many ways. If the support of the fans doesn't mean something to you, you need to have a good think.

The plan for my media conference was set. Kayla and I would be up early, getting the girls ready for an 8 a.m. media conference at the Broncos. It was a lot easier to get organised early when I was a teenager in my first pre-season than it was with two young girls who enjoyed a morning sleep-in. We knew that they would be photographed and filmed after the media conference so we wanted them to be dressed and ready.

The morning went well and I drove to the Broncos excited about taking this step. That was the final test of my decision and there wasn't a second in which I felt nervous heading into the club for the announcement. But I was worried about getting too emotional during the media conference. I had cried when I attended Matt Gillett's retirement announcement. I cried in most sad movies. I cried sometimes when our girls cried. So, it wasn't going to be easy. I had a good plan to help me through – I would get Kayla and the girls to sit out of my eyeline at the media conference so I could read the letter without looking at them. I thought I would cry if I saw them. But best-laid plans have never been my thing.

I felt pleased when I was in the players' recreation room at the Broncos, preparing for the media conference, when some of my current and former teammates began arriving as a show of support. Matt Gillett brought his son, Hunter. Andrew McCullough and his wife, Carlie, were there early. Corey Oates and his wife, Tegan, and daughter, Montana, turned up. Matt Lodge came up from the gym and Alex Glenn came in from a day off. These guys had all meant a lot to me during my career so it was humbling that they would brave the peak-hour traffic for my announcement.

They went in and took their seats in the media conference room while Seibs, Whitey and I waited in the recreation room for one last chat about how the announcement would work. When I walked into the conference room, my plans came unstuck. A large group of Broncos employees had come down for a look, so the room was packed. I was touched to see them because they had been such a great support for me over my fifteen years in the game. Some of them had been helping me when I was a seventeen-year-old without a bank account. That meant the only spare seats available for Kayla, Willow and Romi were in the middle of the front row. Right in front of me. I knew I was in trouble.

Whitey welcomed the group and handed over to me. I quickly thanked everyone for coming and then read from my letter. I got through the first paragraph, then the second and the third. I was feeling good. The fourth paragraph came out easily. And then came the fifth paragraph when I thanked Kayla and the girls. 'Here we go,' I thought. My bottom lip began to wobble and the tears that I shed watching sad movies began to line up, ready for release. I couldn't help but look up to see Kayla and the girls as I mentioned their names. They were smiling at me. Somehow, that was just what I needed. The bottom lip tightened up and I was away. No problems at all. I finished reading the letter and I felt relieved. The job was done.

I was grateful to the many journalists who turned up at a relatively early hour for a media conference. I had tangled with some of them at times but they couldn't have been nicer to me that morning. Their questions were insightful and deserving of thoughtful answers. I was glad that I was relaxed enough to answer them properly. Kayla, the girls and I then went to the training field for photos, and afterwards we headed back home. The morning could not have gone any better. I still had a season ahead of me – and one that I desperately wanted to play well in – but I would approach that with the certainty of knowing when my playing journey in this great game of rugby league would end.

But my final year unexpectedly became the most uncertain of any of my fifteen seasons in the NRL. On the afternoon of our opening match against the Cowboys in Townsville, the COVID-19 cloud began to enclose Australia. Coronavirus was starting to transmit across most of the country. It became apparent that governments would introduce restrictions to stop the spread of the virus and, for a while, our game against the Cowboys was at risk. It wasn't until a few hours before the game that we were told any restrictions would not kick in until at least the following Monday, so we were free to play that night in front of a capacity crowd. But the season was suddenly in doubt. We played well that night, spoiling the Cowboys' opening party at their new stadium with a strong win built on the extensive pre-season work that we had done with Seibs. But that would be the end of normal footy as I knew it. Before our next match, the NRL accepted the medical advice that large crowds could not gather while coronavirus was taking hold. So we won an eerie match against the Rabbitohs at Suncorp Stadium, pushing to a 2–0 win–loss record before the season was placed on hold. I had played more than three hundred NRL games but I'd never had a night like that in an empty Suncorp Stadium. In my first NRL game there fourteen years earlier, I couldn't hear my teammates shouting only a few metres away. That night, I could hear our bench players calling out from the opposite side of the field. The hits were louder, both teams' play calls could be heard across the ground and the absence of any spectators meant that we had to motivate ourselves.

When the season was placed on hold, I wondered if I had played my last game of footy. It was impossible to know what lay ahead as Australia tried to understand the impact of COVID-19. All NRL players were sent away from their clubs from late March through April, leaving us to train at home, following a program sent to us by the Broncos. This was my first glimpse into what life would look like after retirement. I would never be truly ready for retirement, but this forced taste of life without football convinced me that I would be fine after I finished playing. It felt like I was busy every day. But I wanted to play again because I didn't want my career to finish so abruptly.

We resumed the season in late May without crowds but with some rule changes developed during the course of the break. The concept of two referees was abandoned in favour of one – back to how it was when I started my career. I didn't like the change. The game is too busy for one referee to stay across everything. That's why two referees had been introduced in the first place. The single referee was missing things in the ruck, which was understandable because they were also trying to keep the defenders back ten metres. They can't do everything. However, I liked the new rule that an infringement in the ruck would mark a restart of the tackle count rather than a penalty. I also supported the changed rule to allow the attacking team to choose where they set a scrum. The centre-field scrum is a challenge for any team to defend against.

Plenty has changed in rugby league since I started. The players have become much more athletic across my fifteen years, but that hasn't reduced the danger of the little man. Innovations like the scrum clock and fewer interchanges have ensured that the smaller players can still cause real problems in the game, which makes it better to watch. In the end, rugby league is a business. And good businesses have to make their product as attractive as possible for customers in this competitive environment. When business is good, everyone wins – fans enjoy the game more, players get access to better pay and conditions, merchandise sales increase, crowd numbers lift and TV audiences grow. That also means media interest increases, but that's a part of the game that I should have become better at many years earlier. Just like in any profession, some reporters are excellent and some aren't so good. The media provide an avenue to speak with the fans, who are the lifeblood of our game. That's how I look at it. I tell young players that the media are never going away – they're writing about us because people are interested – so it's useful to work out the best way to interact with journalists.

Some of the rookies that I'm playing with in my last season of football will still be playing in a decade's time when they will have their own stories about how the game has changed. If it's changed for the benefit of the fans and the players, then the changes will be welcomed.

CHAPTER 20

The future

DURING MY FINAL SEASON OF FOOTBALL, I WAS ASKED BY A Brisbane school to write a letter to their Year 12 students. The school wanted me to answer one question: if I had the chance to go back in time, what would I tell myself at high school? I could have saved myself plenty of trouble if I'd been able to do that, but there's only so much you can do with advice. It's nothing compared to learning from the mistakes that shape our lives. I have made plenty of those mistakes and I've tried to learn from them, which hasn't been easy, but I've improved over the years.

I told the Year 12 students there were a few things that I would have told my younger self in a heartbeat, including be content with the person that you are. If you can't be happy with yourself, life will be difficult, so go easy on yourself and learn to like the person that you are. That had taken me a long time to work out. I also told the students to set goals and work towards them because they would learn plenty about themselves if they moved out of their comfort zones. That's where so much learning takes place. I also told them that life was too short to be angry and sad – I had wasted a few years doing that. It was always better to be polite and respectful.

But the best advice I could give them came from my journey to rock bottom and back again, starting with my time at the mental health clinic. That visit had helped me work out the answers to some key questions: what did my life mean; who was in my life; what did I need to put into place to improve my life? I learnt many insights at the clinic, but there were five that worked best for me. They continue to work for me. They help me to have a purpose and meaning and to be as happy as I can. These are the tips that I provide to people when I speak about good mental health:

Support network

I learnt this lesson the hardest way possible – I completely shut off my support network, which meant I felt like I was alone when times were tough. Everyone needs a support network – people you can trust and who will be there when you need them. They will tell you when you need to change something. They will tell you when you've done well. They're on the journey of life with you and their support is invaluable.

I've been blessed to have a support network for many years, led by Kayla with great help from Willow and Romi. Throw in Nana, Wayne Bennett, Alex McKinnon, Jan Earl, George

Mimis and others and it's hard to believe that at one point I thought I had no one. They were there all the time – I just had to know the value of their support.

Empathy

Having a kind heart helps us to understand how other people are feeling. It can be easy to get worked up about others, but you never know what someone else is going through in their life. My relationship with my mum was complex but I now know that, while I was angry for many years, Mum was doing it tough. If you can try to understand how someone else is feeling, it helps you to interact with them. Don't forget the power of a random act of kindness – you will get as much out of it as the person you're helping.

Mindfulness

Be in the present moment. This can be vital at important stages of your life. If you're anxious, calm yourself by concentrating on your breathing. Mindfulness isn't always easy to practise but it's very important. There were many times in my past when I desperately needed to practise mindfulness. I constantly had bad thoughts and emotions that overtook me when challenges arose. I remember the times when footy wasn't going well for me and I let negative thoughts take over. Don't mistake mindfulness for meaning you are never emotional. Mindfulness means that reactions to situations are thoughtful and measured.

Exercise

This has never been a problem for me. When I was at the clinic, I enjoyed the gym opening every afternoon at 4 p.m. Exercise is vital for good mental health. It's as simple as getting some fresh air, moving at whatever pace suits you and heading outside your house for a change of scenery. Once my rugby league career finishes, I know exercise will remain a part of my life.

Gratitude

I kept this for last because it's been so important to me. Gratitude has been critical to my life since I arrived at the mental health clinic. Gratitude is one of the four club values at the Broncos. When I walk on to the training field at Broncos headquarters, I go along a corridor that has GRATITUDE painted on a wall from floor to ceiling. It's a great reminder for me. Gratitude is all about giving thanks for the good things in your life. When I arrived at the clinic, I was blind to gratitude. I focused on negative thoughts at all times. But keeping a journal helped me to list the many things for which I was grateful. That meant that, any time I had a setback, I could balance that with the knowledge that I was a lucky person.

My journey through life and through football has been full of moments of gratitude. How can I not be grateful for Kayla, Willow and Romi? After growing up in a very small family – Christmas lunch sometimes included just me and Nana – my own family fills me with joy. Kayla has tried to bring the best out of me for a decade. She is my constant source of inspiration, challenging me to be the best person I can be. We have exciting plans for the next stage of our lives but they will always fit around what's best for our family.

I'm grateful for the love of Nana, who taught me so much. And I'm thankful for reuniting with my mum and for the chance to welcome her back into my life as a grandmother to our daughters. Mum has dealt with her own challenges over the years and I have developed a better understanding of her journey.

Most of all, I'm grateful that my life has turned out this way. What if I had hit rock bottom after I retired? That's a scary thought because the road back would have been far more difficult. Everything happened to me for a reason and I now understand that. I look forward to many years of telling my mental health story to others, hoping that I can help people to learn from my experiences.

If I was able to meet my younger self, I would recommend just enjoying the ride. There will be days of unbelievable joy. There will be days of devastation. But you will get the chance to learn from it all. In the end, the most important thing you will do is to become happy with the person you are. It will take a while, but don't change a thing. The journey, the people, the experiences are a privilege. Embrace them.

Life with Darius

By Kayla Boyd

WHAT'S LIFE LIKE WITH DARIUS BOYD?

The easiest answer is this: the real Darius is so different from the man whom many rugby league fans think they know. He's humble, gentle, genuine, loyal, funny, deep, courageous, understanding and compassionate. He has the quirkiest sense of humour. He has very intellectual conversations and he asks a lot of questions.

He's a doting father. He adores Willow and Romi and they both have him wrapped around their little fingers. And he's the most caring man that I could hope to call my husband.

You've read moments in this book where Darius and I haven't been on the best of terms. There were days and weeks of real struggle between us. But that's part of our ten-year journey. We were twenty-two years old when we met so we didn't have the answers to everything – we had to learn along the way.

When I think of our marriage, I feel empowered and proud. There were times when I felt ashamed and embarrassed. But you have to be completely transparent with each other if you want to move forward. And we have done that.

If we could do our relationship all over again, would we change anything?

Darius and I have spoken about that a lot and the answer we keep coming back to is 'no' – we wouldn't change a thing. Everything has happened for a reason. People can be fixated on the perfect relationship or the perfect marriage, but they don't exist. You have to go through challenging times. Sometimes they're plain devastating times. The test is how you emerge from them.

You know you've got something special when you find that person who wants to fight for you and you want to fight for them. That's us. I wouldn't be who I am and he wouldn't be who he is unless we went through what we went through. We're patient with each other and we want to bring the best out of each other.

Darius and I met on a night out on the Gold Coast over Easter 2010. He was charming, confident, funny and engaging. He was extremely handsome, yet I was most drawn to his confidence. Yes, he was very confident and full of talk that night.

But he lived in another state, I loved living on the Gold Coast, he was a professional footballer and it all seemed a bit too hard. I tried to discourage his interest by finding a reason to cancel meetings between us in the months ahead. But he persisted and I ran out of excuses. I'm glad I did. I got to know an amazing man. That's why I fell in love with him. He was happy. He was always smiling. He was at the peak of his career.

But that was the life Darius wanted to show me. As the walls came down and the resentment built within him, he became a different person. The amazing man I had grown to love changed.

So, who was the real Darius? Was it the man I met or was it this reclusive version? Or was it my fault? I was at such a loss that I wondered if it was me. Whatever the answer, I knew that our marriage couldn't continue in that way. It was unsustainable. Once I accepted that Darius's emotional change wasn't my fault, I could leave our marriage and move on with my life. That decision helped me find the real version of Darius.

He was so brave to seek help and he was so inspiring in the way that he stuck with his plan to change.

Darius really is humble. For all that he has achieved in his chosen career, I have never heard him boast or seek praise or criticise others. I would go to watch him play in front of massive crowds and wonder how this shy, introverted man could handle the pressure of playing in front of so many people. He loved the big stage and he performed so well on it for so many years. He loved playing in front of 50 000 people yet he became nervous when speaking with strangers.

It makes me sad that he's about to finish up his dream of playing rugby league, but he has never been more ready for this next stage after all of the wins, the losses, the injuries, the breakdowns and the breakthroughs. He's given his best for fifteen seasons and he has been professional right until the end.

Rugby league has been good to us. It's enabled us to travel the world. It's helped us to make lifelong friendships. Yes, it's thrust us into the media spotlight and attracted the opinions of people who don't know us, but we understand that's part of high-profile sport. You can't have the upside without expecting a downside.

I get emotional when I think about our story. I cry happy tears about Darius's transformation, especially in the last few years as we've become a very content family of four. Life is so much simpler for us now. We're a happy family and we love each other's company. We have a very relaxed household. Sometimes, though, I wish Darius would get a tiny bit upset about something. That's right. Could he just fire up a little?

I smiled as I wrote that because it's meant in good fun. It's the best sign of the progress that Darius has made in our decade together.

He loves Willow and Romi with everything he has. On game days, he likes to spend most of the day with them and then he'll get himself ready to play. We take the girls to home games and Darius always waves to us as he runs on to the ground. When the game ends he'll take them on to the field for a post-game lap which they love.

I am proud of the man he has grown into, and proud that our girls have a dad like him to look up to. I know he will guide them in the right direction, and he will teach them everything they need to know about resilience and how to bounce back from the hardships that life throws their way. As he says, the comebacks are always far greater than the setbacks.

I never used to take much interest in Darius's career. He liked the fact that he could come home to a place in which football was hardly discussed. In the last few years, though, I've taken a lot more interest in his career. During previous years, criticism of him just didn't affect me. Since we've had our girls, I've felt different and more protective so I've sometimes defended him on social media, to point out the lies and to write about the man I love. I know that some of the criticism of Darius is self-inflicted because of the way he didn't engage with fans for so long. But a lot of it is just wrong. And some of the media stories I've read about Darius over the years are based on such lies that they make me laugh. What else can you do?

I've often wondered how a man who doesn't say a bad word about others attracts so much criticism. That does make me teary. But Darius knows how to block that criticism out. He really is grateful for all of the good things in his life. His mental health talks and his community work have become his therapy. He gets so much out of them.

In the football world, Darius and I are really old. In life, we're very young. Darius has got far greater things in front of him than he's achieved on the football field. Football was the first chapter. He'll do incredible things. He'll keep enriching the lives of others and he'll keep telling his story in the hope that it helps someone else.

People who spend time with Darius always leave feeling better about themselves. He has that effect on everyone he meets. I hope you feel the same way after reading his book.

Kayla

Acknowledgements

Darius Boyd

Wayne Bennett wrote in the foreword that he doesn't know what I would have done if it wasn't for rugby league. I've thought about that over the years and I don't know how my life would have panned out. I know for sure that I wouldn't have completed this book.

My sincere thanks to my manager of twelve years, George Mimis, for his friendship, support and his guidance through this project. To the team at Hachette, my thanks for doing this so well and with such ease, especially during a football season. Thank you to all of my previous coaches, teammates and club officials who gave their time in this process.

I hope the book itself serves as an acknowledgement to the many people who have helped me along my journey in life. I'm grateful for all of the help that has come my way, from my junior career to the incredible support provided during my most challenging times.

To Michael Crutcher, thanks for your support over the last five years and for taking on this project. I know we've had many conversations over those years that came in handy for this book. I'm grateful that you took it on and did it so well.

To Kayla, Willow and Romi – we've come a long way. You bring me joy that I can't describe. I can't wait for the years ahead.

Michael Crutcher

In almost three decades in journalism and business, I have spent time with many well-known people, from prime ministers to premiers, CEOs, rock stars and plenty of high-profile athletes. None intrigued me more than Darius Boyd. I found him genuine, honest, warm, deep and incredibly humble. It's been a privilege to help Darius tell his story.

My sincere thanks to Darius, Kayla and George Mimis for trusting me. Thanks to Vanessa Radnidge, Jacquie Brown, Meaghan Amor and the brilliant team at Hachette.

Thanks to my team at 55 comms including Alec Camplin and Clancy Nugent for their expert research.

To the many who have so generously helped me during this time and over the years – David Fagan, Robert Craddock, Bart Sinclair, Trevor Marshallsea, Scott Thompson, Michael Westlake, Adrian Haines, Ben Dorries, Paul Malone, Shane Rodgers, Edward Davidson, David Barber, Darren Bullock, Steve Lansley, Terry Tracey, Russell McDonnell and so many others.

And to my dearest wife Ainsley and our boys Bill, Dash and Sam – I can never thank you enough for your support and love. And for being so patient.

Resources

If you are struggling please reach out to someone.
Admitting I needed help changed everything for me.
There are some contacts here for you. – Darius

Lifeline Australia
13 11 14 for 24/7 crisis support and suicide prevention services
www.lifeline.org.au/

Beyond Blue
1300 224 636 for 24/7 crisis support and suicide prevention services
www.beyondblue.org.au/get-support/national-help-lines-and-websites

Kids Helpline
1800 551 800
kidshelpline.com.au

MensLine Australia
1300 789 978
mensline.org.au

Suicide Call Back Service
1300 659 467
suicidecallbackservice.org.au

Headspace
1800 650 890
headspace.org.au

QLife
1800 184 527
Qlife.org.au

AUSTRALIA

If you would like to find out more about Hachette Australia,
our authors, upcoming events and new releases you can visit
our website or our social media channels:

hachette.com.au
HachetteAustralia
HachetteAus